BEING HUMAN IS HARD: CHOOSE FORGIVENESS

The Power of Connections, Courage, Compassion, and Creativity

BY CHRISTY HEACOCK, PhD

DEDICATION

*Dedicated to the forgiveness heroes who
shared their stories with me and all those who
have the courage to choose forgiveness*

ACKNOWLEDGEMENTS

I am deeply grateful to the forgiveness heroes who shared their stories with me so others could learn from their experiences. Thank you for your generosity! Thanks also to the many people who guided me to the forgiveness role models I interviewed and provided me with support and encouragement.

My critique group members, Karen Hall, Marsha Ahrenkiel, Ken Eisenbraun, and Donald Mease were instrumental in supporting me and helping me move from academic writing to writing for all people interested in learning more about forgiveness. Your expertise and feedback were extremely valuable.

The committee chair for my doctoral dissertation, Dr. Susan Marcus, provided excellent guidance on how to conduct qualitative research plus was a source of inspiration and support as I completed my PhD. I will be forever grateful for your wise counsel and belief in my project.

I am extremely grateful for my family and friends. My husband, Roger, has sustained and encouraged me throughout the process of researching and writing. My daughter, Jessica, gave me excellent feedback and allowed me to share stories about her to illustrate experiences with forgiveness. My daughter, Ashley, a writer herself, helped provide resources, and answered my many questions regarding the use of technology.

I appreciate all the people who have forgiven me when I have messed up and needed grace. You have shown me the way to forgiveness and given me the support I needed to become more courageous, compassionate, and creative. Being human is hard but forgiving and being forgiven makes it much easier.

CONTENTS

Introduction

BEING HUMAN IS HARD: CHOOSE FORGIVENESS

*The secret of change is to focus all your energy, not
on fighting the old, but on building the new.*
—SOCRATES

I t's hard to be human. We're always messing up, making mistakes, offending and being offended. If the stuff we humans do to each other isn't enough to distress us, we have the never-ending threats of disease, natural disasters, geopolitical conflicts, and accidents to add to our insecurity. How can we stop feeling angry and bitter about the painful things that happen to us and deal with the people who hurt us? How can we live with past regrets and failures and attain peace of mind? How can we accept an imperfect world and quit attacking ourselves, others, and God for all the undesirable things that happen in it? The answer—choose forgiveness.

In order to choose forgiveness, we first need to understand what it is and what it is not. Forgiveness is *not* excusing, condoning, or ignoring bad behavior. In fact, it's the opposite. Forgiveness means having the courage to uncover and confront our pain so we can let go of destructive thoughts, feelings, and behaviors and move beyond shame, guilt, anger, and resentment. Once we understand forgiveness, we can move on to deciding whether or not we want to forgive.

Why choose forgiveness? Choose forgiveness because genuine, true forgiveness produces better mental and physical health, improved communication and relationships, and personal and spiritual learning and growth. We become relaxed instead of tense, smile instead of frown, love instead of hate. We spend time working on gratitude rather than plotting revenge, we problem solve instead of blame, confront injustice rather than ignore it. Forgiveness transforms our lives as we move from victims to heroes in our life story.

Saying yes to forgiveness means saying no to seeking revenge or retreating in shame. Deciding to forgive, however, is just a first step because *emotionally* forgiving a major offense is not automatic or instantaneous. We may choose forgiveness, and even say we've forgiven, but still have a hard time truly feeling it deep down. How do we obtain the ability to genuinely forgive ourselves and others?

4 Cs: Connections, Courage, Compassion, Creativity

For my PhD dissertation in research psychology, I interviewed people from different religions, backgrounds, ages, genders, and situations and found that what they all had in common was the ability to forgive through the power of 4 Cs: Connections, Courage, Compassion, and Creativity. Spiritual, religious, and social connections helped guide and support the people who shared their stories with me. That guidance and support gave them the courage to confront and uncover their pain, helped them compassionately understand the offensive event, and aided them in creating a new chapter in their life story. The 4 Cs empowered them and led to what they described as liberation, freedom, a lightened burden, an expansion of space, and the cleansing of their hearts.

This book is a compilation of the incredible stories that they and others so kindly agreed to share with you. Throughout each narrative, I highlight how each person uniquely used the 4 Cs in the forgiveness process. Their hope, and mine, is that the stories we share will help you, the reader, gain insights into how to use the 4Cs in your own life. I prepared The Forgiveness Experience diagram that follows to summarize the similarities I found in the experiences of my study participants, and to give you an overview of what forgiveness meant to them and could mean for you.

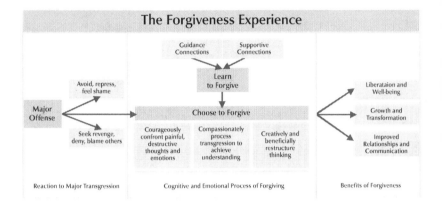

Forgiveness is a Universal Virtue

Human beings have been struggling with forgiveness issues throughout history. Our instincts emphasize survival and we're wired for "fight or flight," *not* for loving our enemy. But we have needed cooperation, not just competition, in order to survive. Therefore, we have the ability to feel empathy for others and to use our higher order thinking skills to settle disagreements peacefully and productively.

The world religions all extol forgiveness as a virtue and provide sacred scripture to inspire and guide us. Christianity's Lord's Prayer (Matthew 6: 11-12, New Living Translation) reads, "Give us today the food we need, and forgive us our sins, as we have forgiven those who sin against us." Islam's holy book, The Qur'an (4. 35) instructs, "Repel the evil deed with one which is better, then someone with whom you were divided by enmity will become like a bosom friend" (as cited in Freke, 1998, p. 79). Hindu scripture, Ramayana, Yuddha Kanda 115 advises, "A noble soul will ever exercise compassion even toward those who enjoy injuring others or those of cruel deeds when they are actually committing them—for who is without fault?" (as cited in Freke, 1998, p. 78).[1]

Scriptures from the major religions tell us that personal transformation is only possible when evil is met with goodness. Anger and retaliation are viewed as imprisoning an individual in self, whereas forgiveness recognizes the essential unity of humankind in the oneness of God or what is deemed sacred.

Classic literature from the ancient Greeks debated the meaning of forgiveness and questioned the utility of revenge. In Homer's *The Iliad* (8th century BCE), characters who had sought revenge and hurt each other were able to recognize their common humanity and similarities and reach what the Greeks referred to as *syngnome*, which means "an understanding." Aristotle's *Nicomachean Ethics* (4th century BCE) focused on the virtues of justice, truth, and generosity and noted the need for syngnome, as human nature was described as often ignorant of wrongdoing or affected by stressful conditions.[2]

Throughout this book I will be referencing spiritual texts, literature, and scientific research on forgiveness, as well as my research findings and my own personal experience with forgiveness. You will be introduced to thirteen people (with fictitious names) with ten different sacred belief systems who described to me their experience with forgiveness of at least one major offense. "Major offense" was defined as a painful transgression or event involving self or a significant relationship. Offenses included murder, torture, parental abuse, racism, and betrayal.

The eight women and five men I interviewed, whose ages ranged from 25 to 76, were all living in the United States at the time of the interview, but had varied backgrounds and situations.

Despite having different self-described sacred beliefs—which included Agnosticism, Bahia, Buddhist philosophy and spiritualism, Christianity, Islam, Judaism, Lakota belief in Sacred Pipe and Red Road, Shirdi Baba follower, Syncretism (meaning the combination of different forms of belief), and Tibetan Buddhism—the amazing people I interviewed all described forming connections that provided them with the courage, compassion, and creativity they needed to forgive.

Become a Forgiveness Hero

I call my study participants Forgiveness Heroes because it's time we broaden the definition of what it means to be a hero. Patty Jenkins, director of the fantasy superhero film *Wonder Woman*, stated, "Our fantasy of a hero is that he's the good guy who is going to shut down the bad guy." However, she warned, "There is no bad guy. We are all to blame." She felt that "new kinds of heroics need to be celebrated, like love, thoughtfulness, forgiveness, diplomacy ... No one is coming to save us."[3]

The heroes in this book will come in the form of forgiveness role models who were able to:

- struggle with painful emotions
- take responsibility for their thoughts and behaviors
- let go of destructive judgments and desires

- pursue justice and accountability without vengeance
- adapt to unpleasant realities in a compassionate, creative manner.

The people you will meet in this book transformed their thinking in a manner that led to expanded insights, peace of mind, and compassionate, respectful behavior toward self and others. They did not wait for a "hero" to come and change things to comply with their personal beliefs about the way their offenders and the world should be. They became their own heroes, empowered by the 4 Cs. I hope their stories will encourage and inspire you as much as they have me.

Forgiveness Heroes (names are pseudonyms)

NAME	AGE	SACRED BELIEF AND CULTURE *(all living in the United States and born in the U.S. unless otherwise noted)*
Anna	25	Agnostic; born and raised in Norway
Basel	31	Muslim; born and raised in Africa
Ben	36	Christian (Protestant)
Esther	72	Syncretic: Ancestral, Christian (Protestant and Catholic); Sufism, Buddhism, Lakota spirituality
Fadel	38	Muslim; born and raised in Iraq
Jacob	72	Jewish
Katherine	76	Christian (had attended both Catholic and Protestant churches)
Lisa	29	Spiritual (raised Buddhist & now follows it as a philosophy more than a religion)
Mo Chou	40	Tibetan Buddhist; born and raised Christian in China
Ria	39	Devotee of Indian spiritual master Shirdi Sai Baba (Hindu/Muslim); born and raised Catholic in Croatia
Rose	66	Belief in Sacred Pipe and Red Road; Lakota heritage
Valerie	66	Baha'i
William	70	Christian; born and raised on Pine Ridge Indian reservation

WHAT DO YOU MEAN BY FORGIVENESS?

Before we sit down to talk, let us define our terms.
—VOLTAIRE

What is forgiveness? It's not an easy question to answer because there are varied interpretations. Even though forgiveness is considered a virtue, we still sometimes think of it as wimpy and cowardly. We worry about people getting away with something, taking advantage of us, and acting badly with no consequences.

My daughter Jessica called me one night, very upset with her roommate (whom we will call Melissa), to whom she was subletting her apartment. For Jessica, subletting her apartment meant she could meet the total cost of her monthly rent without going in debt. No sublet, no meeting expenses.

"Mom, I can't believe this. Melissa just told me she is moving out, but it's three months before her lease is up. How am I going to find a new roommate for that short time period? Plus I'm so, so busy. I don't want to deal with this."

"I can certainly understand why you're upset," I sympathized. My daughter had been dealing with a variety of stressors and didn't need one more.

"I'm so mad! Melissa doesn't seem to realize this is frustrating and stressful for me. She found a place that's a little cheaper, but she probably won't save any money because I'm keeping the security deposit. She's clueless! I don't even want to talk to her."

My normally pleasant daughter didn't want to be very compassionate or nice to her roommate. "Melissa needs to know what pain and discomfort she's creating for me. She needs to know breaking the lease is not right!"

Forgiveness Is NOT Condoning, Excusing, or Overlooking Bad Behavior

People need consequences or their bad behavior will likely continue. In cases of abuse or oppression, condoning, excusing, or overlooking would simply mean the abuse or oppression would be allowed to continue.

So what does forgiveness mean? First, it means confronting the hurtful event and all the feelings that come with it. My daughter was justified in being upset. Who wants to spend time and money dealing with a frustrating situation created by a broken promise when she could be reading a good book or enjoying happy hour with friends?

Overlooking or excusing her roommate's bad behavior would mean Jessica's anger would be buried somewhere in her subconscious, only to surface again at some embarrassing time. Or it might stay undercover while insidiously raising her blood pressure. On the other hand, if she becomes outraged and intent on revenge, she could embarrass herself with inappropriate behavior, and anger would still take a toll on her health.

Thankfully there was a middle way.

Acceptance and Understanding

Forgiveness means accepting that something happened that you did not like, and also accepting whatever feelings the incident manifested in you. When things go wrong it's natural to feel angry at ourselves, at others, at God or fate. We can view anger as an alarm that alerts us to the possibility of danger or the need for change. Our task is to understand why we're angry and to process our justifiable—or unjustifiable—anger in a productive manner that will lead to personal well-being, better relationships, learning and growth. Some things are fairly easy to forgive and won't take long to process. Major issues, however, generally require guidance, support, hard work, and time.

My daughter's roommate situation would generally be considered a minor offense. I say generally because people perceive things differently based on their experience and personality. For some very defensive people, it could be a major offense, and for other really laid-back individuals it may not even show up on their radar as offensive. My daughter considered it a minor trespass but, as mentioned, she wanted to be sure her roommate received consequences.

Jessica talked about her feelings, controlled her initial angry emotions, and then worked to morally and compassionately understand the issue at hand. I asked my daughter why she thought Melissa broke the lease.

"I think she's going through a difficult time and may be depressed. She's young and wants to become an actress, but she's finding out it's a super tough business. She may be so caught up in her own problems she doesn't realize her decision to break the lease was selfish and inconsiderate."

Morally, Jessica decided the right decision would be to communicate her unhappiness with the behavior, but not seek revenge or try to retaliate. To maintain integrity, she needed to make a decision that creatively pursued fairness and learning for all concerned. How could she move forward without bitterness, and what could she and her roommate learn from the event?

Jessica could not find a new roommate quickly so, in order to meet her expenses, she kept Melissa's security deposit, an action that Melissa did not like. But the decision was fair and it was a lesson for Melissa regarding the consequences of breaking a lease. My daughter had to accept the fact that she had less gym time and social time because of the situation, but she received valuable lessons about communication and structuring rental agreements.

We can forgive when (a) a hurtful event is **courageously** confronted; (b) **compassionately** and morally processed so understanding is reached; and (c) **creatively** resolved in a way that allows safe and productive forward movement. Notice there are steps involved, and time, and effort. You may be thinking, "Isn't there just a pill to take or at least easier steps to follow?" Sorry, no.

Forgiveness Rewards

But there are rewards if you learn to be more forgiving! You will be more at peace—mentally, physically, and spiritually healthier. You will have better relationships with improved communication and feelings of safety. Plus you will be learning and growing, not repressing or blaming, actions that get you nowhere because you're locked in your own dark prison of negativity.

The people you are going to meet in this book agreed that forgiveness was letting go of destructive thoughts and emotions that impede growth through an effortful, compassionate, moral, and transformative process. They were very enthusiastic about forgiveness and willing to share their stories because they felt that forgiving had given them freedom, lightened their burdens, and transformed them in a very positive way. Their beliefs and role models inspired them, and they realized the joy that comes from living life without resentment and bitterness.

Forgiveness comes easier to some persons than to others, but it is rarely easy if the transgression is major. If an offense is small, forgetting may be a good option. But if a transgression is painful, trying to simply forget—meaning to overlook or pretend it doesn't matter—won't work.

If we are indeed hurt and confused by a wrongdoing, be it our own or that of another, courage is needed to face the shame, embarrassment, fear, or pride that is blocking forgiveness. We may need to become vulnerable and question our assumptions and beliefs. Perhaps we need to question or confront someone more powerful than us and we fear criticism or losing the support of significant others. In those cases, religious, spiritual, or social connections are needed to provide guidance and support.

We don't have to do tough stuff alone. Indeed, we probably need to admit we cannot do it alone.

Before Forgiveness Feels Good, It Feels Hard

The people you will meet had forgiveness role models that included people from the past and present who had guided and inspired them. As they became skilled at forgiveness they also served as role models for their family, friends, and community. Forgiveness feels good, and so does helping others. But before forgiveness feels good, it feels hard.

Pain can fuel our development and transform us if we work to understand it and use it for growth. But it takes time to process whatever is hurting or haunting us. If you try to forgive too quickly you may simply be ignoring injustice, abuse, genuine feelings, and truth.

Forgiveness Cannot Be Forced

A warning: forgiveness can be approached in the wrong way. Pressuring someone to forgive can backfire and make a situation worse as people repress anger or feel shame because of their genuine emotions. Pressure to forgive may be instigated by a more powerful party that wants to continue oppression or abuse and quiet those who are hurting. Forgiveness may be urged onto someone by family or friends who are uncomfortable with conflict and don't want to upset the status quo. "Just get over it," they may say, with their interests in mind, not yours.

We ourselves may be motivated to overlook an offense if we wish to avoid conflict and keep the peace. We may choose to go along with an unjust or unfair situation when it seems to be the best solution. People stay with abusive spouses for the sake of the children or don't challenge the boss because they can't afford to lose their job. A pertinent question is, "Will speaking up and challenging authority or the transgressor lead to positive results or just make things worse?" Sometimes it's not clear if we're being selfish or courageous when we contest what we perceive as unfair. Picking our battles is an act of discernment.

Confronting Injustice

Overlooking injustice is not forgiveness. Accepting the fact that injustice occurs and courageously looking for compassionate and creative ways to improve a situation is, however, part of the forgiveness process. Sometimes there is very little or nothing we can do about the situation that is making us angry except change our attitude toward it. At other times we need to summon up our courage and actively work to change a dysfunctional situation.

German priest Dietrich Bonhoeffer, before dying in a Nazi concentration camp, warned against cheap Christian grace being used to allow injustice to remain.[4] Voltaire, a satirist from the Enlightenment era, is quoted as saying "I like to sin, God likes to forgive, really the world is admirably arranged."[5]

The concern that forgiveness may indicate weakness or avoidance of confronting justice issues was illustrated when a white supremacist killed nine persons in a Charleston, South Carolina, church Bible study in 2015, and some persons in the congregation offered forgiveness swiftly. That action was praised by many, but criticized by those who believed being quick to forgive meant ignoring an unfair, racist system and missing an opportunity to pursue justice.[6]

Positive forgiveness results can only be achieved when honest emotions are uncovered and justice and mercy are pursued at the same time. Until we understand a transgression and feel that we are moving forward in a fair, just, compassionate manner, we will be unable to let go. And that is good, because condoning, excusing, overlooking, or simply trying to forget bad behavior is not healthy. Painful feelings can lurk in your subconscious, surfacing in dysfunctional, hurtful ways.

Work on forgiveness with your head, but listen to your heart. Only then will you know if you are truly on the path of forgiveness.

JUSTICE, MERCY, AND HUMILITY: ALL AT THE SAME TIME

He has shown you, O mortal, what is good. And what does the LORD require of you? <u>To act justly and to love mercy and to walk humbly with your God</u>.

—MICAH 6:8 NIV

Micah 6:8, in the Old Testament Bible, states that what is good and what the Lord requires is "to act justly, to love mercy, and to walk humbly with your God." So is Micah offering us a multiple choice decision? Is the answer (a) act justly, (b) love mercy, (c) walk humbly with your God, or (d) all of the above?

If we want revenge or punishment only, we may pick (a). If we hope to condone or excuse a transgression, (b) might be our choice. If we don't want to confront a problem we may choose (c) and let someone else worry about the justice and mercy part. If we truly want to be forgiving, we pick the toughest choice—(d).

Balance Justice with Mercy

The human brain likes to simplify and generalize, which is an efficient, fairly easy way to think. Things are right or wrong, black or white. You are for us or against us. People are either good or bad. However, when we pick choice (d), we are challenging our mental abilities because we have to balance justice with mercy. When we walk humbly, we have to look inside ourselves and become aware of both our strengths and our weaknesses, our own capacity for both good and evil.

When someone hurts or disrespects us, it's natural to look for negative aspects of their personality. The same goes for groups. Psychologists call that *confirmation bias*. We look for information that confirms our opinions of an individual or a group, and we find what we're looking for. When someone is nice to me, I look for positives. When they're mean to me, I look for negatives.

I realize I sometimes get irritated with people who have offended me when they act nicely. Darn it—I want them to always do the wrong thing so I can judge them harshly and feel smug and self-righteous about my superior ways. I don't like it when they mess up my simplistic, self-centered thinking by doing something kind or intelligent. If I don't recognize and correct my bias, I will ignore my offenders' good behaviors or cunningly turn everything they do into something bad. If I'm aware of my thoughts and my biases, I can upshift my thinking and remind myself that we humans are all a mixture of saint and sinner, capable of great good, but often falling short because being human is hard.

There is no algorithm for forgiveness, which means there is no certain, step-by-step path that will always lead to a happy ending. Forgiveness requires discernment, examining different perspectives, and challenging assumptions and expectations. We need **courage** so we can confront unpleasant truths, take responsibility for our feelings and actions, and adjust to change. We need **compassion** in order to empathize with someone who has hurt us, or to forgive ourselves for an event we deem unforgivable. We need **creativity** to find purpose in our pain that inspires us to write a new, redeeming chapter in our life story.

Let me introduce you to Basel, a young man who was able to balance justice and mercy and remain humble. He was strong enough to forgive the person who tortured him and who had played a leading role in the death of his close friends.

THE COURAGE TO LOVE YOUR ENEMY: BASEL'S STORY

You can't forgive without loving. And I don't mean
sentimentality. I don't mean mush. I mean having enough
courage to stand up and say, "I forgive, I'm finished with it."
—MAYA ANGELOU

Basel was a 31-year-old scholar who studied politics as well as the Quran. He grew up in a devout Muslim family. His religious values, as well as his democratic political principles, were very important to him. Basel was active in a movement to improve the government of his country, and his political activities led to his imprisonment, interrogation, and torture. When stability was restored to Basel's situation through successful revolutionary efforts, he was able to forgive the person who imprisoned and tortured him and who was part of the government responsible for the death of a close friend who died in his arms.

Basel described his interrogation and torture, which was euphemistically, sardonically, called "the party" by the torturer. Basel explained, "The 'party' took place in a very small, tiny room with one chair. I sat there on the chair and they handcuffed my hands to the ground, put a chain on my neck, and tied the chain to my feet to keep me always looking down and bending my back. My head was facing into my knees the whole time of interrogation. Of course, that was humiliating."

The interrogator started the questioning with the following warning, "Here is the deal. There are three things you cannot say: no, I don't know, I don't remember."

"So every time I mentioned one of those three phrases," said Basel, "he was torturing me even more. I was peed on, hit in the face, beaten, and forced to attend the 'engagement party.' The engagement party consisted of putting two rings on my fingers and connecting them to electricity so I would receive shocks. 'Engagement on the beach' was when they added water to the mix."

Basel was arrested several times and the "party" continued as described above each time. He was held for approximately two weeks at a time in a cell the size of a dining table for six people. "My cell had dirt walls and was very tall, very dark. The floor was filled with water. They wanted to torture you even in your cell and kept you standing up in the middle of the cell the whole time because you couldn't sit or sleep in those conditions. Of course, after some time, no one cares anymore about the dirt and the water. I was so exhausted and tired that many times I just lay in the water and against the walls."

Faith in God helped sustain Basel, and Basel let his interrogator know he believed his just cause would win in the end. In response, the interrogator replied, "If your God came down here to help you, I'd put him in the next cell. I'm capable of doing anything to you right now. I literally can fuck you, physically. I can kill you, and I can let you go. I can do anything to you."

Justice and mercy were both very important to Basel, who had a strong moral identity. Despite being arrested and tortured, Basel continued to take risks in order to help create a free, just society in which there was equality and dignity for all, not just a few. His beliefs would be tested, however.

The revolutionary movement Basel was involved in continued and became more successful at the same time as the interrogator rose up in the governmental regime's hierarchy. The governmental response to the change movement's advances was to crack down on the revolutionaries even harder. Basel described a defining moment in both the revolution and his life.

"I was crossing the bridge to the town square during a peaceful protest and the police, who were now under the command of the man who had tortured me, started shooting at us. I got a bullet in my leg, and my friend, who was running next to me, was fatally shot. I couldn't help him, though I tried. I held him in my arms and he looked into my eyes."

"I'm dying," he said. "Leave me here and keep going. I've lost my life for this, please go and don't waste my life for nothing. Win this."

"I'm so sorry, I will go. I will get your revenge," Basil responded. "I promise I will get revenge. I will never let your blood go for nothing."

At this point Basel's friend, who became his hero, said, "Please don't waste your energy on revenge, just keep our dream alive. Work for our principles."

"I was just so mad," Basel explained. "I was letting my anger lead me, but my friend's words were a wake-up call. That was the moment I knew sticking to our principles was the right thing to do."

The protest cost the lives of 1,500 revolutionaries, five of whom were Basel's close friends, but it led to changes in the power structure. The revolutionaries took charge, the tables were turned, and Basel found himself with authority over his interrogator. Moral choices had to be made.

"We were sitting at a table close to each other. So that was the minute, the time, the moment when I could do anything to the person who had tortured me. He once was a powerful giant. Now he was broken and didn't know what was going to happen to him. He knew we could shoot him in the streets like an animal, or we could put him in prison for life, or we could create a revolutionary court and try him as a war criminal for crimes against humanity. He was terrified."

Basel was committed to justice and he was also committed to mercy. He was careful to remain true to his principles and religious values because he did not want to become cruel and hateful like the person who had abused him. He explained, "The Quran teaches me that if you respond to the hateful with hate, hate will never stop. Hate will keep going."

Compassion for a Torturer

A belief in compassion inspired Basel to sympathize with his torturer. He observed his offender and realized the man was always insecure, worried, nervous, and fearful of betrayal; unable to enjoy his power, money, or family because his negativity was controlling him. "I felt he was a poor guy. I looked at him like he really, really needs help. From my experience with him, he was always worried, always wondering. He always had this weird feeling he was not safe, and he wondered which one of his friends would betray him."

Basel was physically tortured in prison, but Basel's torturer was also tortured in a prison—a personal prison he had created in his own mind. During interrogations, the government official had tried to find out more about Basel's friends and had confided to Basel his cynical, personal thoughts on friendship. "You think this wallet [referring to himself] has friends? There is no such thing as friends. They will betray you the first chance they get. No one loves you. No one is faithful."

The torturer was acting out of fear, and Basel understood this meant his torturer believed he was doing the right thing in order to secure safety and security. As the interrogator was leaving the negotiation room, Basel told him, "Everyone will have free and public trials. You will be held accountable, but we are not going to torture anyone. I will never forget what you've done to me because that's my history. That's my experience. I will keep it in my mind so I keep working to stop this from happening to anyone else. But I absolutely forgive you, and I have nothing against you, and I love you as a person."

So how could Basel tell someone who had tortured him and had a role in his friends' deaths that he forgave him and even loved him as a person? Basel understood many horrible, hateful actions are taken because people are hurting, afraid, and ignorant of the true ramifications of their behavior. Basel told his torturer, "I know you may have believed that was the good thing to do, the right thing to do. But that was wrong. You have made a mistake and you will be held accountable."

Forgiveness Means Freedom

I asked Basel what his major forgiveness experience meant to him now. "It set me free. I don't spend any time thinking about how to take revenge. I don't waste my energy on anger or madness. I use my power, time, and thinking to do good for me, for God, for our community, for an environment in which people don't hurt each other. Forgiveness set me free."

Basel learned to walk humbly, with God's mercy and justice leading the way, not his own hurt and pain. At times, Basel and his friends were tempted to use violence to counter violence, so they developed a slogan to inspire them and help them persevere: *Our peaceful movement is stronger than their bullets.*

Forgiveness is a Struggle Within Yourself

I asked Basel what his greatest impediment to forgiveness was. He replied, "To really feel the forgiveness. It's good to say to someone, 'I forgive you.' But your heart may still be saying, 'Ugh, why did I do that?' Having forgiveness both inside and outside, that's really a struggle. I won't lie to you. When I saw this guy [the torturer], my mind and heart were telling me, 'You, son-of-. ....' I see forgiveness as strength, and you're only weak when you punish people. Forgiveness is not a struggle with the other person; forgiveness is really a struggle with yourself."

Basel made the decision to forgive based on his sacred beliefs and moral principles, but deep, emotional forgiveness is an effortful process. Basel had to control angry feelings and an instinctive desire to simply punish harshly. I asked him how he did that and he said, "I had to work to forgive myself for forgiving. When I forgave my torturer my heart was telling me, 'I will never forgive you for forgiving that guy.' But I gave myself that forgiveness for forgiving him and worked to achieve that peace level that we should all struggle to reach."

The part of Basel's brain that reminded him of his religious values and cultural principles (his cerebral cortex) had a hard time keeping his amygdala and limbic system (the parts of the brain that control short-term survival instincts) under control. When we have been hurt, it's natural to want to lash out, fight or flee, instead of upshifting our thinking so our behavior matches our moral values.

In addition, much of our learning is observational because we are equipped with mirror neurons that allow us to learn through imitation. We instinctively mimic the behavior of others, which works well when we are young and need to quickly learn how to adapt to our environment. It's a great way to learn when we are surrounded by admirable role models. Unfortunately, it can backfire when the behavior we are observing is objectionable.

Hurt people often times simply copy the behavior of the person hurting them, which helps explain why revenge seems to be so popular. You call me a nasty name; I'll call you a nasty name. You hit me, I'll hit you back. Never mind that I find those things morally wrong and, as Gandhi is famously quoted as saying, "An eye for an eye makes the whole world blind."

Basel had the courage to confront the uncomfortable emotions he was feeling, and do battle with the part of him that wanted revenge and vindication. He worked to understand his offender with compassion.

Self-compassion was also needed, because Basel's dangerous activities and actions had caused hurt for his family and friends, which saddened him and generated inner struggle. I asked Basel what helped him persevere and write a new chapter in his life story.

"The first thing was considering all facts that related to my principles and the work I have done. Yes, I have hurt so many loved ones, but at the same time, I have changed so many people's lives—people who were in prison, or tortured, or had bad living conditions. I never did any of this for me. I always was working for other people. So I solved this struggle within myself by remembering that I worked for people, and there is a big reward for that, but also there is a price for that. The second thing that helped me was the support I received from people. I had negative reactions to my work, but also backing from people who believed in what I'd done and knew the good I'd done."

Overcoming Hurt and Guilt

Gratitude for the positive support from people in his life and for his accomplishments helped Basel rise above the hurt and guilt he felt. In addition, when times were tough and he was losing hope, the examples of role models who had endured suffering while practicing forgiveness guided and strengthened him. "I connected my story to what happened to the Prophet Mohammad when he started inviting people to follow him. He was jailed; his fellow friends were tortured and killed. He was exiled and his family suffered a lot because of his message. Nelson Mandela, one of my heroes, was in prison for twenty-seven years. Martin Luther King, Jr. and Abraham Lincoln, also my heroes, were assassinated."

I asked Basel how he would describe the relationship between forgiveness of self and forgiveness of others. He responded, "You need to achieve peace in yourself first before you can really do it outside. We all can lie. We can pretend. But we cannot fool ourselves."

Basel was able to work for justice, show mercy, and walk humbly with God. How does a person walk humbly with their God? Humility means openness to accepting and recognizing one's own weaknesses and strengths. It means overcoming feelings of inferiority and superiority so you have the courage to rebuke injustice when needed, along with the wisdom to realize you are no better or worse than the person committing the unjust action. The harmful behavior becomes the focus of condemnation, not the person.

It's hard to act justly, AND love mercy, AND walk humbly with your God, but when you are finally able to forgive and know you are staying true to your moral identity, you may get to experience peace, comfort, and what Basel called a natural high.

"I've been on both sides of the aisle and I can tell you that every time I feel negative energy, I have a headache, my hands are shaking, and my face gets red and hot. Every time I forgive, I feel so peaceful and comfortable and a smile pops onto my face. It makes me high."

Basel understood that forgiveness has the power to make us feel better mentally, physically, and spiritually. When we stay true to our moral identity, we feel good about who we are and who we are becoming. We have every right to be angry and upset when we are treated with cruelty and disrespect, but living a life of bitterness and resentment isn't good for us or the people we love. Choosing forgiveness means striving for a way of life that brings you peace and self-worth—a natural high.

WHY SHOULD I FORGIVE IF IT'S NOT MY FAULT?

HEALTH, RELATIONSHIPS, AND GROWTH

"We must develop and maintain the capacity to forgive.
He who is devoid of the power to forgive is devoid of
the power to love. There is some good in the worst of
us, and some evil in the best of us. When we discover
this, we are less prone to hate our enemies."
—MARTIN LUTHER KING JR.

Forgiveness is not easy, but I contend it's better than the alternative. Martin Luther King Jr. recognized that we will all disappoint each other and ourselves at various points in time because being human is hard. We behave badly because we are ignorant or can't control our emotions. When we are at our most difficult to love, we may be most in need of love. The beauty of love bursts forth when it is embracing us in all our imperfection.

Research psychologists strive to be scientific, meaning we work to control bias, try to be objective, and seek to replicate findings before declaring confidence in them. The personal health benefits of forgiveness have been replicated in many studies,[7][8][9][10] plus researchers have found that organizations profit from the positive, learning-focused culture that forgiveness creates.[11] Psychologists have joined with theologians in the study of forgiveness because the mental and physical benefits of forgiving are impressive.[12]

Genuine forgiveness leads to positive results. The people I interviewed described three general areas of improvement in life: personal health, relationships with others, learning and growth. If you're wondering if you've truly forgiven, you can ask yourself the three questions that follow.

1. **Do I feel healthier mentally, physically, and spiritually?**
   Look for improvement, not a carefree existence. Forgiveness doesn't mean your life becomes easy, it means it becomes eas*ier*. Better blood pressure, sounder sleep, fewer headaches, more smiles, greater joy, and a lighter mental burden are signs of forgiveness. The better you get at forgiveness, the better you will feel.

2. **Have my relationships and ability to communicate improved?**
   Do I feel more loving and compassionate? Have I been listening more? Do I feel more accepting of human weaknesses, my own and others? Have I established boundaries with people capable of hurting me? Do I feel safe?

You may have had to end a relationship in order to improve it if you were being abused or in some way hurt—or being hurtful or abusive yourself—and couldn't find a way to change that. Forgiveness should only mean reconciliation if mutual respect and safety have been achieved. Relationships are always works in progress so expect bumps in the road that make new construction necessary. You may need to do maintenance and repair work as you create the next chapter in your forgiveness story.

3. **Have I learned from my experience?**
There is a song by Jason Gray I like called "Learning" with the lyrics, "If I fall, I win, every time I get up again, 'cause I can't lose if I keep learning." When we go through tough times we often grow spiritually. Spiritual teacher Eckhart Tolle is quoted as saying, "For most people, their spiritual teacher is their suffering. Because eventually the suffering brings about awakening." Some people who have major forgiveness experiences call them transformational because the insights and awareness gained are so significant. The main thing is—keep learning.

I've been on mission trips to five different countries—Lithuania, Nicaragua, Peru, Israel/Palestine, and Kenya. When I returned people asked me if it was a life-changing experience. On my first trips I said, "No, but it was a wonderful experience and I gained a lot from it." I said no because there wasn't a dramatic shift in my thinking. My last mission trip was to Kenya. This time when I was asked if the trip was life changing I said, "Yes, all my experiences are life changing. I just keep growing and learning."

My journey has not been a dramatic, amazing shift from unforgiving to forgiving. It's been a slow, often hard climb, and I'm still struggling to reach the top. But I do remember certain moments when insights finally came to me that made my life easier and allowed me to forgive. I'll describe one for you.

My father had significant anger problems that affected me and others in my family negatively. I'd think, "He should be a better dad. He should handle things responsibly and maturely." I cleared myself of responsibility for any arguments we had by thinking, "He's the parent and I'm the child. He should know better than me. He should be wise and loving."

Did you notice all the "shoulds" in my thinking? I was full of them. Did you catch that all the shoulds pertained to my dad? He was the one who should change. I was the victim—the child of an abusive parent. Poor me.

I wish every child had a wise, mature, loving parent who could manage their anger and love their children unconditionally. However, I started looking around and realized there were kids a lot worse off than me. I read *A Child Called It*. I read lots of history and biographies. Wow—did I learn that life can be tough.

I started changing my shoulds into wishes. I could of course wish I had a dad like the ones described in Hallmark Father's Day cards, but since I didn't, all the shoulds I was uttering were worthless. I needed to learn how to deal with an angry dad and I needed to be grateful I had wonderful grandparents and a nice mom. As an adult, I learned to set boundaries, understand my dad's weaknesses, and appreciate his strengths. He was intelligent, hardworking, and could at times be very funny and thoughtful. I couldn't change my dad, but I could change my thoughts, which changed my emotions and behaviors. I traded my victim identity in for that of a creative problem solver and started improving the story I was writing for myself.

THE JOY OF LEARNING

Knowledge is a wrapped gift.
It is expectantly waiting for us,
But unable to show its contents
Until the season is right and we are ready and able to open it.

I'm an educator and there is nothing more rewarding than having students who love to learn. Don't all students love to learn? I think all students have the potential to love learning, but sometimes we mess that up by rewarding performance and obedience instead of curiosity and the willingness to try and fail.

Carol Dweck is a researcher and professor known for her work on goal orientation theory and the effect of a growth versus a fixed mindset on motivation. She initially examined goal orientation's effect in academics, but expanded the theory out into social and moral domains.[13]

Goal orientation theory describes two general categories of goals: learning and performance. A learning goal orientation is seen as a desire inside of us to obtain personal growth and master challenges. A performance goal orientation is based on doing things correctly with a focus on pleasing or impressing others and avoiding punishment.[14]

Great goals motivate us and there is nothing wrong with either learning or performance goals. Unfortunately though, if we are overly concerned about performing, we may have trouble forgiving ourselves for the inevitable mistakes and wrong turns that come with learning. We may worry so much about living up to our own or others' expectations that we are unable to accept the predictable bumps and bruises that come with mastering new tasks. We want success and we want it now.

If we can't forgive ourselves for what we perceive as failures, we may look for others to blame, and charge them with messing up our lives. Or we may turn on ourselves and feel we are losers with a capital L, so we load up on shame and pity instead of patience, determination, and creativity.

In the case of my dad and me, I wasn't performing the way I felt I should be in life, and I felt one cause of that was that my dad was not performing the way he should be performing in life. I was intent on fixing the blame, not fixing the problem. What I needed to do was take responsibility for my weaknesses and failures. I couldn't learn and grow until I owned my problems. I'd just be whining and complaining, and the world didn't need more of that, nor did I.

If we can focus on the joy of learning and accept the fact that we and the people who disappoint us are born to learn, not perform, we can adjust our expectations and work on figuring out the puzzles in life. We can let go of the anger that comes when we are upset with people (ourselves included) for not performing according to the standards we have constructed in our minds. We can use our energy to optimistically embark upon a time of reconstruction and growth.

That leads us to a question and another area of research undertaken by Carol Dweck. Is our ability to learn and grow fixed and difficult to change, or is it malleable and affected by our environment?

Forgiveness Means Openness to Change

Dweck found that individuals who believe abilities and capacity for change are fixed are unlikely to put forth effort and persist in achieving challenging, difficult tasks. They view chances for success as limited and failure as likely. Persons who have a malleable, optimistic view of the capabilities of self are motivated to engage in a challenging, steady process they believe will lead to improvement and learning.[15] [16]

Forgiving is effortful and requires a belief that change is possible. We need to believe, "I can face the shame and anger I'm feeling. I can find a moral, compassionate way to deal with my dilemma. I can create a new way of thinking, feeling, and behaving."

In addition to believing people can change, forgiveness requires believing that we are not defined by our mistakes. Albert Ellis, a cognitive psychologist, found that individuals tend to rate themselves and others holistically and overgeneralize.[17] For example, when we or others act in a way that we perceive as wrong, we may categorize the whole person as bad instead of confining our judgment to the act of which we disapprove. A situation with both negative and positive aspects may become totally awful and disturbing.

Some behaviors are horrendous and despicable, others just ridiculous or irritating, but whatever the magnitude of the offense, nothing is gained by giving yourself or others devilish horns and a derogatory label. Making mistakes is a natural part of being human. Learning from our mistakes can make us happy to be human.

ENHANCED COMMUNICATION
AND PROBLEM SOLVING

Fix the problem, not the blame.

Whose fault is it? That's a question often asked when a mistake or ill-fated event occurs, and it indicates we are looking for someone to blame and probably hoping, perhaps assuming, guilt will fall on the shoulders of others. Fixing the blame may make us feel better if we are able to exonerate ourselves, but our relief may be fleeting if the problem remains. A more productive question is, "Why did that happen?" The answer to that question will be focused on the circumstances that caused the problem.

If our focus is on who to blame, the parties involved may get caught up in defensive moves and denial because no one wants to bear the burden of blame. If we are marked as the person at fault, the consequence may be punishment, shaming, or—in our litigious society—an outrageously expensive lawsuit. Ouch! No matter who is at fault, the goal of blaming is often discharging pain and discomfort onto another, not fixing the problem.

If our focus is on fixing the problem, we may still wish to establish fault, but only so we know how to move forward toward a solution to our difficulties. The goal is learning how to improve. We want to prevent offensive, hurtful, unproductive actions and situations in the future.

Forgiveness Is About Problem Solving

Forgiveness is all about problem solving. Something has happened that we don't like and we need to figure out how to deal with it. Forgiveness issues often times are not our fault—someone else is to blame—and our anger is legitimate and understandable. The process of forgiveness is about moving past blaming and shaming and on to fixing the problem. It's about using our anger energy to fuel creative solutions to what is ailing us.

Sometimes we become paralyzed by shame and deny we are hurt and embarrassed, even though deep within us toxic pain is lurking. Denial and avoidance don't solve problems. Repressing our true feelings about how we were treated or what happened to us means our anger energy is sizzling inside us, which can lead to health problems and passive aggressive behavior. Passive aggression means we find sneaky ways to get back at people we are afraid to confront directly.

Forgiving means viewing our pain and discomfort as a signal that change is needed. What kind of change? That's where the problem solving comes in. Forgiving people are courageous, compassionate, creative problem solvers. They aren't bullies and they aren't wimps. They are hard workers because life requires fixing challenging problems.

You may quickly *decide* you are going to forgive an offense, but forgiving a major offense should never be swift because it takes processing time. Forgiving is often described as "letting go," but we can't and shouldn't let go until we have learned from our painful experience and feel safe enough to move forward.

Forgiveness Doesn't Justify or Condone Oppression

Some forgiveness problems are very hard to resolve and therefore very hard to forgive. I visited Palestine and Israel several years ago and spoke with a diversity of people who expressed different perspectives regarding the conflict that has been going on since 1948, when what Palestinians call the Nakba, or the catastrophe, occurred. The nation of Israel was formed to provide a homeland for the Jewish people, who had suffered horribly in Europe, both during and before the Holocaust, which was the atrocious culmination of anti-Semitic hatred. Unfortunately, what was gain for those of the Jewish faith became loss for many Palestinian Muslims and Christians who lost their homes and many of their rights.

I spoke with Michal, a Palestinian Christian in Israel, and asked what forgiveness meant to him. He explained he equated forgiveness with weakness and avoidance and stated, "We cannot forgive when an injustice happens over and over. I cannot forgive when Israeli soldiers continue to abuse us and the Israeli

government continues to issue and enforce laws that oppress us."
(personal communication, September 14, 2015)

Sometimes forgiveness is urged onto people who are oppressed
or treated unfairly by those who are benefitting from the status
quo—be it on a governmental or a personal level. If the 'F' word
has become toxic to a person or a community because of its
association with injustice, words describing forgiveness such
as empathy, humility, and dignity for all may do a better job of
conveying its meaning and producing a beneficial result.[18]

Meaning Is In People, Not Words

Many years ago I was advised that, "Meaning is in people, not
words." When I first heard that bit of wisdom it didn't fully regis-
ter with me. Words are concrete and tangible. We can look them
up in the dictionary and establish their true meaning. We can
argue with words, and assume that those we are arguing with
are defining words in the same way we are. Or they certainly
should be if they're not, right? Well ... I find it very difficult to
fix a problem if I forget that words are symbols that I interpret
according to what *I* believe, what *I've* been taught, and what *I*
think should be.

I remember listening to a conversation between two friends,
one of whom was adopted. The woman who was not adopted
knew the other woman's adoptive mother was named Beth, but
she was inquiring about whom the woman's *real* mother was. The
conversation was turning into an argument because the woman
who was not adopted was solidly assuming that a real mother was

the woman who biologically gave birth to a child. The woman who was adopted was horrified that her friend would insinuate that the wonderful woman who raised and nurtured her was not her *real* mother. Both rigidly clung to their personal definitions of what was real. The conversation went something like this:

"So who is your real mother?"

"Beth is."

"No, I mean who is your *real* mother?"

"I just told you. Beth is."

"But I thought you were adopted. So who is your real mother?"

"My real mother is Beth."

Communication was going nowhere until I suggested the possibility of different interpretations of the same word. I said, "I think for some people, a real mother is the woman who raises and nurtures the child, whereas others think of real in terms of biologically giving birth." They then clarified their terms and the conversation moved forward.

Real communication involves going beyond words that may be misconstrued and probing for the meaning those words represent. Real communication solves problems.

Deciding to forgive means deciding to listen and understand a different point of view. It means figuring out ways to get along with others and determining how to calm the chaos in our heads and hearts. When we forgive we courageously and compassionately confront our pain and hurt, work to understand it, and then creatively transform it into growth and new life.

So why choose to forgive even though it's not your fault?

Choose to forgive so you can tear down the roadblocks preventing healing and growth and construct a better life. Choose to forgive because it is morally the right thing to do and because you want to solve a problem that has been hurting your health and relationships. Choose to forgive because you want to embark upon a journey filled with courage, compassion, and creativity. And remember, you don't have to do it alone.

OKAY, I'LL GIVE FORGIVING A TRY. HOW DO I DO IT?

THE 4 CS: CONNECTIONS, COURAGE, COMPASSION, AND CREATIVITY

Everyone thinks forgiveness is a wonderful idea,
until they have something to forgive.
—C. S. LEWIS

There are many pathways to forgiveness and it's important that we choose a route that is right for us. Religion and spirituality can help lead us to forgiveness, but the sacred beliefs that guide us will vary based on our own special needs and the people and culture that surrounds us. Therapists, family, friends, and organizations may or may not have the ability to aid us on our journey. We need support and guidance as we learn to forgive, but we have to search for it and discern what will work for us.

The **connections** we form with others and/or the divine will be beneficial if they empower us with courage, compassion, and creativity. We need nonjudgmental support and guidance as we uncover our genuine feelings and examine our hurt. Support and guidance give us the **courage** to take responsibility for how we will choose to move forward.

Compassion means empathizing with others and making ethical choices that match our moral identity. **Creativity** opens our minds to fresh perspectives and helps us envision a healthier way of thinking and behaving. Forgiveness is all about **transformation**. We take our pain, our scars, and use them to craft an inspiring new chapter in the story of our lives.

Find Connections for Guidance and Support

Wise people don't spend time jumping through other people's hoops. Wise people don't spend time creating hoops for other people to jump through. Wise people learn how to dance with hoops and create circles that inspire, include, and enrich others.

I wrote the above quote one day as I was reflecting on our interconnections with each other and the transformations that can take place when we cross paths. We are all connected. Some of our connections may help lead us to forgiveness; others may discourage forgiving or make it more difficult. How can we find those wise people that create healthy circles that will inspire us and facilitate our ability to forgive?

Often times we look to religious institutions, and they can be awesome places to find support and guidance. However, because forgiveness is difficult and human beings are good at finding what they believe are excellent excuses for not being virtuous, it's possible they will disappoint. I remember participating in a Bible study discussion of the words of Jesus in Luke 6: 27-28, "But to you who are listening I say: Love your enemies, do good to those who hate you, bless those who curse you, pray for those who mistreat you." A dear, sweet, elderly lady with a troubled look on her face said, "I don't think people were as mean and awful in Jesus's day or he wouldn't have said that." She must have forgotten about the bloody, brutal Roman crucifixions and public stonings in Jesus's day.

It is very hard for human beings to love everyone because we tend to look at competitors or those who are different from us as enemies or bad people. Joining a religious group may help you forgive, but if you're not careful it could make you unforgiving of those people who do not believe as you do. People have shown an amazing ability throughout history for taking sacred scriptures and using them to justify revenge, vindictiveness, and violence toward others.

Persons interpret scripture in different ways and individually emphasize different aspects of their religion. One religious person may emphasize warmth values such as love, forgiveness, and humility. Another may prefer conscientiousness-based virtues such as justice, responsibility, and reciprocity.[19]

Persons of the same faith view God differently. Some may perceive of a punishing God that plays favorites and expects perfection, while others may view God as more merciful, inclusive, and accepting of human imperfection.[20] These evaluations will determine how a person applies religious principles to personal forgiveness behavior.

Many people are uncomfortable with religious institutions because they have been hurt or disillusioned by judgmental, hypocritical, self-righteous members of those institutions. If that is the case in your situation, there are other groups you can turn to. They may be spiritual, cultural, therapeutic, or social. However, don't expect to find a perfect fit because being human is hard and we are all in need of forgiveness. Do look for people who will accept you as you are, whom you can identify with, who bring out the best in you, and who make you a more loving person when you are around them.

At times it may be that you can't find any supportive human beings to guide you. This is the time to seek a higher power and to believe, if you don't already, in God, angels, or some kind of sacred, loving, and forgiving life-force. Then say over and over, with your whole heart, my favorite one word prayer, "Help!"

The next person you will meet is William, an amazing man who grew up with blatant racism and the resulting hate that discrimination and disrespect inflames. His was a long, hard journey to forgiveness that he credits to some remarkable role models.

THE IMPORTANCE OF ROLE MODELS: WILLIAM'S STORY

Don't worry about anything, but pray about everything.
With thankful hearts, offer up your prayers and requests to God.
—PHILIPPIANS 4:6

Forgiveness is universally seen as a virtue, but revenge is cruelly satisfying and is a popular theme in tough, hunky-guy movies. If your role model is a gorgeous woman or handsome guy who gets even with bad guys and shows them who's boss, it may be hard to figure out why forgiveness would be a desirable option. And indeed, if you're good at getting what you want in life and feel self-assured, and especially if you feel self-righteous, you're probably not all that interested in learning about forgiveness. Not at this point in your life anyway. Motivation to forgive comes when factors like high blood pressure, inability to sleep, headaches, uncontrolled anger, angst, and, in extreme cases, prison time come to call.

The people I interviewed all had role models that helped guide them to forgiveness. Role models can be family members, friends, historical or present-day people we admire. Role models need to walk the talk, not just talk the talk. Role models also need to be people with whom we can personally identify.

William was a 70-year-old grandfather who grew up on an American Indian reservation. He and his family suffered humiliation and poverty because racism was rampant, and the trauma they experienced was soul wrenching. William grew up seeing his family shamed by white people who told them their culture was bad and needed to be destroyed. "Kill the Indian, save the man," was a motto used to guide the government's administration of reservation boarding schools for children who were often forcibly removed from their parents. Signs in the windows of businesses stated, "No dogs or Indians allowed." Bitterness and hatred toward white people in general led William down a road filled with violence, alcoholism, and broken relationships. His hatred grew into rage and expanded to other minority populations and finally to his own tribal people who didn't hold the same beliefs he did. William spent time in prison, went through five marriages, and hung out exclusively with friends who he said "scurried around in the dark like vermin."

So how did William find the light? It took lots of effort, but William was tough, smart, and resilient. He became a recovering alcoholic and a spiritual seeker who found a home with Christianity, putting to rest his bitterness toward the Catholics who had controlled boarding schools on the reservation. Helping others overcome alcoholism and anger became William's focus, and he put on workshops for the United Methodist Church. The church was impressed with his abilities, and selected him to serve on various committees. His participation in one of those committees guided him to the role models who would inspire his forgiveness journey.

William identified as Christian, but he couldn't identify with Jesus as his forgiveness role model. Maybe that was because of Western culture's depictions of Jesus and Mary with lily white skin or the descriptions of Jesus as "king" and "lord." What could a white guy, especially one whom the Catholics controlling the reservation boarding school called a king, know about prejudice and oppression? Jesus as a forgiveness role model works better when you realize he was a Palestinian Jew, part of a minority severely oppressed by the Romans, and a man betrayed by friends and followers.

The historical trauma suffered by American Indians was, unfortunately, at least as bad for African Americans. William served on a church committee with black pastors. Those pastors had suffered worse racism and trauma than he had as an American Indian. William heard personal stories of black family members being murdered in the Jim Crow South with no consequences for the white people who had committed the crimes. One black pastor had been forced to watch helplessly as his sister was tied up, set on fire, and burned to death. William pondered, "How do you *not* hate white people after that?"

So William asked the black pastors that question. "How do you not hate? How do you forgive?" The advice they gave focused on two behaviors, "Talk about your pain with other people, and pray about it."

Just talk and pray? That advice didn't make sense to William at first. Gradually, however, he came to understand their counsel and recognized its similarities to the 12-step program of Alcoholics Anonymous. William was a recovering alcoholic before he became what he called a "recovering racist." He realized that talking and praying about pain was a key to dealing with outrageous injustice and gut-wrenching regrets. It could lead to understanding and acceptance. It could lead to the awareness that you are not alone and that there is hope for the future. It could lead to love and forgiveness.

Forgiveness led William away from the high blood pressure that was destroying his eyesight, away from sleepless nights, away from a continuing cycle of hatred that threatened not only him but his family. Forgiveness provided him with a second chance and an opportunity to become a role model for his grandchildren.

Acquiring a New Identity

William realized he needed to put forth effort if he wanted his new, moral, Christian identity to guide him. "I got myself two hats," explained William. "One says "Warrior for Christ" and another has three crosses on it. I posted the Ten Commandments in my vehicle so I'm reminded of what is important when I'm taking my grandchildren to and from school. When I feel unforgiving and need help, I think of the black pastors, read the Bible, and go talk to my pastor and people in my church."

William's daughter, whom I'll call Mary, didn't have the benefit of being raised by the forgiving William, but she was fortunate enough to be loved by the forgiving William in adulthood. Mary was an alcoholic, and one day while she was shopping at Wal-Mart she started a loud tirade against her father, accusing him of being a child molester. William admitted that when he heard about Mary's actions, the unforgiving, angry man he had once been would have responded violently and vindictively. His daughter was not only shaming and hurting him, she was putting him in danger from others who might want to punish him for his acts if they believed Mary's false accusations.

But William's new identity led him to examine his natural instincts and justifiable rage. Mary's actions were hurtful and her accusations untrue, but William knew inflicting more hurt would not lead to good results. He reminded himself, "She doesn't know any better. She's ill. She's got a disease and I've got to pray for her."

William knew what to do in that difficult situation because he had been guided by role models and had become skilled at forgiveness. "I put her [Mary's] name on a prayer list at church and it's amazing because she's calming down and she's sobering up. I started talking a little bit more about it with my pastor, and all of that made a big difference, especially the talking and the praying. So I told her I loved her and I'll be darned if she doesn't tell me she loves me now. But it could've gotten really bad had

I not had enough patience or some idea of what to do. I mean I could've gone over there and just slapped the snot out of her. That's what I would've done 20 years ago if somebody said that to me. I'd just go kick the shit out of them. And if I couldn't kick the shit out of them, I'd hit them in the back of the head with a two-by-four. I'd get them one way or another. I'd get even. Even over things that didn't need to be gotten even over."

Controlling Anger

Anger should be a warning sign, not a state of mind. Anger alerts us to cognitive dissonance, meaning what's happening is not matching up to what we think should be happening. For example: that car should not be cutting in front of us; our co-worker should not be telling lies about us; our spouse should not be having an affair with our best friend; racism should not exist in the world.

Anger as a warning signal is an important survival mechanism that alerts us to danger and the need for change of some kind. Anger as a state of mind gives us high blood pressure and increases our chances of acquiring heart diseases and other physical ailments. Anger means we have been hurt. Hurt because life is not going the way we expect it to, and it makes us so darn mad, often justifiably so.

William did not eliminate anger. Instead, he learned to manage his anger so it would work for him, not against him. He calmed himself through self-talk and putting transgressions into perspective.

"I've got to go through that intra-personal dialogue in my head about what's going on. I've got to take about 40 seconds to identify the cause of my anger and realize that okay, this person made a choice, I made a choice, and it's not the end of the world. I have to tell myself that, to reassure myself. I may feel like it's the end of the world, but it isn't. When I feel like it's the end of the world, that's just my grandiosity and delusional thinking kicking in. It's not like that for real."

In addition to putting a distressing event into perspective, William used empathy and humility to calm himself. He became accepting of the fact that human beings, including him, mess up a lot. "I tell myself, how many times did I do what that person's doing? Understand it. They've probably had a bad day. They don't need me making it worse. So I've got to talk myself down."

Instead of seeing individuals as either good or bad, William looks at them as having strengths and weaknesses. He looks at himself that way too. He works on his weaknesses and also works to emulate the strengths in others that he would like to have. "In order to forgive a human being, I've got to be able to let go of my weaknesses—my anger, my vindictiveness, my resentment—and then see the good in the other human being. The qualities that they have that I want to possess."

William, like others who have experienced historical trauma, also needs to decide how much of his family or group's pain he is carrying as his own personal burden. "I've got to decide if my anger and my rage go all the way back to my childhood, to the first time I started learning things. Is this racism real or imagined? Is it stuff that came from my parents, my grandparents, aunts and uncles? I have to decide and look at that and say no, this doesn't belong to me. I don't have to be angry about that. That isn't my life. It doesn't relate to me."

Talk and Pray

"What would you say to someone who's experienced a painful transgression or event and was considering forgiveness?" I asked.

"First of all, follow the black pastors' advice. You can always pray about it and you can always talk about it."

William lets people know, "If you want me to pray with you, I can pray with you right now. Then if they're interested they can talk to me about what's going on with them. If not, I ask them to find somebody they're comfortable with. It doesn't have to be me. Talk to anybody and pray at any time, wherever you are. Sometimes people will say they don't know how to pray, and I say that's okay. All you've got to do is talk to God like he's standing next to you. Tell him what's wrong with you. What you want to change. How you want to feel differently. That's all you have to do. That's prayer."

Sometimes life gets so tough forgiveness seems impossible. If you're a proud, rugged individualist, you may think you need to face problems on your own. But being human is hard, and we were made to care for each other as we journey through life. We need help maneuvering through difficult terrain.

The next person you will meet, Ria, discovered the power of forgiveness through a spiritual source because human support was not available. Ria's spiritual source strengthened her enough so that she, in turn, could give guidance and support to her family members. One purpose of learning to forgive, is for giving to others.

SPIRITUAL COMFORT AND EMPOWERMENT: RIA'S STORY

Forgiveness is the key to action and freedom.
—HANNAH ARENDT

When I interviewed Ria, she was attending an Ivy League school in the United States. She was a very talented, passionate, well-educated and well-traveled woman in her 30s from Eastern Europe. She'd had a successful career in local politics and had often been in the media. To the outside world, she was the epitome of success. But her worldly success had not been able to make up for her inner emotional turmoil, which several years ago had become too much to bear.

Ria's tipping point came at the age of 32, when she gave birth to her second child. She was having difficulties in her relationship with the child's father, who was in the midst of a long, messy divorce. She was also subconsciously holding on to unresolved childhood pain, which needed to be uncovered. Something had to change. If Ria wanted to continue to be a strong woman that others could lean on, she needed to find a source of support for herself.

"My mother wasn't my stepping stone. She didn't have the character to support me. She was dependent on my stepfather, and when I had issues with him she would always take his side—even though he did some horribly abusive things to me. She wasn't there for me. I carried that with me subconsciously because when you're a child, you bury those things you don't understand. But my buried pain would rise up, and I couldn't be nice to my mom."

Ria explained that her mother and father divorced when she was very young. Her father then found a new family to which he gave his emotional and material support, and he neglected Ria. Ria's mother remarried, but unfortunately, the man she married abused Ria. Ria's mother was subservient to her husband and did little to protect her daughter, therefore creating pain and hurt that Ria carried with her into adulthood. After Ria's stepfather died, her mother felt helpless and became dependent on alcohol.

Problems with her family relationships and internal confusion prompted Ria to seek a new spiritual path that began in India. "My stress somehow led me to leave for India. I don't know why, something just pulled me in that direction. I went to India for almost four weeks. I was advised by an astrologer I knew to first find a Nadi reader (a person who reads palm leaves) so I went to the internet and found one."

The Nadi reader made some predictions about Ria's life, many of which had already come true when I interviewed her. The most disturbing information Ria was given was the prediction that her mother would die in 5 to 6 years. This shocked Ria and led to a change in her perception of her mother. She became determined to aid her mother and prayed, "Let me help her with her alcoholism. I don't want her to die having problems. I don't want to be at my mother's grave knowing that she was an alcoholic. I want my mother to die happily connected with herself and with God. I just want to be there with a great feeling; happy for her that she's found peace. I don't want her soul wandering somewhere—wherever—unhappy."

Sometimes we are stubborn about forgiving because we feel the other person should change, not us, and we are waiting for them to do so. We often have high expectations for the type of relationships we want with our parents and other family members, so disappointment with family can create high hurdles of pain difficult to surmount. When we realize time is limited, our motivation to forgive may increase.

Ria was Catholic by birth and when she was younger she would go to a church and pray. "But," she explained, "I never had a connection with the priests because I didn't like the way they were preaching religion. They were saying one thing, but they were living and doing something else. Because they seemed like hypocrites, it didn't really connect me to my religion."

A Secure Spiritual Source of Comfort

What changed when Ria went to India? "I read a book about this saint called Shirdi Baba, an Indian spiritual master who lived about 100 years ago. When I started reading, I also started to cry. It was as though this person from the book was talking to me directly, like he knew me. I started connecting to him, and I went to the place where he lived 100 years ago and I stood at his grave. I just surrendered myself. I said 'Listen to my problems and protect me.'"

Shirdi Sai Baba died in 1918 and was known for teaching the importance of love, forgiveness, service, charity, contentment, inner peace, and devotion to God. He is quoted as saying, "Everyone's God is one," and he did not believe in distinguishing between religions and castes.

Until Ria connected to Shirdi Baba, she had not experienced a secure attachment in her life. Secure attachments provide people with the confidence needed to accept human failures, and explore and develop without fearing separation from others or the divine. Significant people in her life had not been able to provide her with the emotional anchor she had needed.

"I was in the dark, always looking for somebody, and I just got more disappointed every day. I would complain, 'Why don't you have time for me? Why don't you listen to me?' I was looking for comfort in other people and that's wrong. You should find comfort in yourself, and once you find peace, you can then help others."

Ria found in Shirdi Baba a secure spiritual source that could guide her and support her as she became more forgiving. "There was nobody else that I had been able to lean on or get attached to until Shirdi Baba, and the connection grew stronger and stronger the more I practiced my faith. I chanted, said mantras, read his books, and wrote about him. He would bring people into my life who helped me, and he provided me with answers to my problems in dreams."

One of those dreams led her to receiving a full scholarship to an Ivy League school in the United States. But before her life became easier, it became harder.

Uncovering Subconscious Resentments

Ria had inner anguish and resentment she needed to let go of. A healer in India told Ria, "You have a lot of problems and emotions you're keeping in your body. You think you've solved your problems, but unfortunately, you have just repressed them."

We tend to repress thoughts and feelings that give us cognitive dissonance, meaning what we are thinking and feeling doesn't align with what we believe we *should* think and feel. We may also repress painful feelings that we are simply unable to deal with at a certain time in our lives because we do not have the mental and emotional resources necessary to cope with them. Repression can be a short-term solution to an overwhelming problem, but if disturbing feelings are buried too long, the consequences become apparent. Health and relationships suffer and growth may be stunted.

Repression is tricky because it's a subconscious process. We repress without conscious awareness and, because repression's purpose is protection, we deny we are doing it. It often takes a supportive relationship to boost our courage and guide us as we let down our defenses and uncover our pain.

Ria had told herself that she had forgiven her abusive stepfather before he died. "My stepfather died a really horrible death from cancer. He lost about 40 pounds and was a skeleton in the end. When we were burying him I cried and said 'I forgive you,' but I didn't. I repressed it. But when I was told I repressed it, I said, 'No, no.'"

When Ria became confident enough to confront her true feelings, she was able to free herself from the horrible pain that had been locked inside her. She said, "I could finally breathe with a full heart and full lungs. Forgiveness is an underestimated word. Learning how to forgive is learning how to be happy."

Resolving Issues on a Heart Level

I asked Ria what role religion and spirituality played in her ability to confront her true feelings and forgive? She responded, "It's number one. It's at the top." Ria questioned whether anything other than religion and spirituality really allows us to let go and feel free. "We can go to a psychiatrist and maybe resolve some issue on a mental level, but spirituality resolves issues on a heart level. With spirituality it can be so transformative, so life changing. You feel that somebody takes your heart and cleans it. Cleans it, cleans it, cleans it and that's the only way that you can actually go forward. Or you can go to a psychiatrist plus have religion. I think a combination of both is great."

Ria's connections with healers in India and her spiritual attachment to Shirdi Baba gave her the courage, compassion, and creativity needed to forgive. In Ria's case, she also felt very connected to her family. Her wish was to guide and support them so they could find the inner strength and spiritual support needed to genuinely forgive themselves and others.

Forgiving is For Giving

Ria felt moved to bring her mother to India and help her heal. "I had to prop my mother up and give her the strength to actually start valuing herself. It was difficult because my mother had been unable to guide and support me, but I needed to find the ability to help my mother deal with her issues."

Ria admitted she was amazed she had the internal fortitude to help her mother who, at first, refused to go to India. But Ria was firm and told her mother, "You know what, you and I might be arguing in this life, and we might be at each other's throats the whole time. We may have trouble connecting, but on the soul level I have to help you, and you have to pack your things and we have to go. I'll come pick you up and put you in the taxi. We don't have to talk all the way. We don't have to talk in India, but you're going to have to come."

Ria's mother then kept quiet and went to India. She also kept drinking, and was imbibing whisky on the plane the whole trip. Mother and daughter had a loud argument at the airport, but

Ria's mother made it to the healer. After three weeks of cleansing, she stopped drinking and started praying. She read the Bible, gained a mantra (a word or sound repeated to aid concentration in meditation), and went to church. Ria described the change in her mother. "She's functioning and working, but with a different vibe. Now we have great communication and whenever I can, I give her support."

I asked Ria why she decided to work so hard to not only forgive her mother, but also help her mother overcome her problems. "I think that your mother is like the main focus in your life. She's the one who brings you into this world. She's the one who carried you for nine months, you came through her. If you don't have a clean, pure connection with that person then nothing will be okay, because there is a reason why you came through that organism."

Ria believed her own healing was tied to her mother's healing. Ria's sister disagreed at first and was full of resentment toward their mother. But Ria advised her sister to rise above her pain. "Don't look at it in a shallow way. Go above all these things and look at your mother as the soul that brought you into this world. Don't just think about what she's done to you. Learn to forgive and feel compassion in your heart."

Ria was able to bring her sister and mother together for meditation and therapy. Now her sister and mother visit each other, talk, and have a good relationship. "The important thing is to be willing to work on understanding each other. We feel comfortable with each other now, and we don't look for ways to escape communicating."

Forgiving her mother and establishing a respectful, loving relationship with her meant that Ria could be a moral, family-oriented role model for her own children. She said, "I have a good relationship with my mother and I want my children to have a good relationship with me. If they saw that I was always fighting with my mother then I'm sure in ten years it would be the same thing with us—just a replica because they would pick up our habits."

Thinking about the afterlife motivated Ria to spread forgiveness to family and others in need. "It's just being aware that there is a next life. I believe the soul goes somewhere and the more you forgive, the less baggage you'll carry with you. With hatred and constant negative judgment of others, you're creating this lower energy inside of you. People who hate become ugly because inside of them they're always criticizing, and never happy with anything. It manifests physically, and I don't want to die like that."

Forgiving can be for giving. Ria explained that when she strengthens herself and cleanses herself of baggage, she has more energy for giving to her family and others. "It's like my husband and kids can put their fingers on me and get charged up. I can light them up."

Staying Spiritually Charged

Ria realized that if she was going to be a forgiveness energy source for others she needed to keep her batteries charged. "I cannot just be immersed in my family because they take a lot of my attention and then I cannot focus on myself. So in the morning I always need an hour and a half for myself. Sometimes my husband says, 'Why do you need so much time? Why do you have to do it in the morning?' And I say, 'If I don't do this, I won't be a good wife. I won't be a good person. I just need time to reflect.'"

In addition to setting aside time, Ria set aside a place in her home that she entered for comfort and inspiration. She created an altar where she put pictures of her family and Shirdi Baba, as well as Jesus Christ, because Shirdi Baba advised people not to renounce the religion they are born with. Flowers, fragrant candles, and food also helped create a positive, pleasing energy. Ria made sure she prayed during both good times and bad times so her spiritual connection could stay strong.

Ria's spiritual connections provided her with a shield of courage and compassion that protected her from the extreme pain she used to feel. "I'm not alone anymore. I don't get internally destroyed anymore. I don't allow the problem to enter, and that's why there's no need to forgive anymore."

"No need to forgive?" I responded. "What about when people aggravate, hurt, and disappoint you? What about all the injustice and oppression in the world?"

"I still cry when I see a sad movie or observe something that is unfair. I'm often the first one to cry, it just comes out. I might get angry and say 'Oh my God.' I might yell and tell people they can't do certain things. But I'm not devastated, so the problem—the negativity—doesn't come deep inside me. I believe that people come to me for a reason. I share my problems with Shirdi Baba and say, 'Those people who have to stay, let them stay. Those who have to go, let them go—just always protect me. Be there for me.'"

When Ria had trouble forgiving, she turned to prayer and often felt she received the spiritual message "be patient." She said, "I have learned to really appreciate every single day and to appreciate people who come into my life. When problems come to me I tell myself, 'They're not problems, they're opportunities.' I've learned how to deal with them in a much softer way, a nicer way, and with a bigger smile."

Ria stressed the importance of finding a spiritual connection that speaks to you. "I know there's only one force and that is God. The way God appeared to me was in the form of Shirdi Baba. But it doesn't matter how you talk to God. Find your spiritual connection and dedicate yourself to it. I don't pray just when I feel sad or am mourning. I want my protectors to be with me when I'm happy, too, because then I really become connected. I involve them in my life at all times."

Forgiveness Means Freedom

"How has forgiveness changed you?" I asked Ria.

"It gives me freedom. It really gives me satisfaction and happiness. It gives me wings to fly. I feel lighter because I don't have baggage regarding my mother and many issues. I can be freer for my children. I'm looking forward, not backward."

But what if you're locked in a situation you don't have the financial means to escape? Most of us can't afford to go to a different country for spiritual healing.

Seeking Supportive Connections—Durah and Craig

I talked about forgiveness with a group of women in Kenya, some of whom were dealing with depression as well as resentment and hopelessness. They were all struggling financially. One woman, whom I'll call Durah, talked to me after my presentation and explained that she had unknowingly contracted HIV/AIDS from a man whom she had worked with. Unfortunately, her family blamed her for the situation. To make matters worse, Durah had quit her job because it was too hard for her to continue working beside the man from whom she had contracted the disease, especially since he took no responsibility for her condition. She was very depressed and didn't know how to forgive herself or the man who gave her the virus.

I so wished I could give Durah a pill or some magical advice that would make things better for her quickly. But I couldn't make her disease go away or force her family and friends to understand her pain. There are no easy answers to difficult situations, but there are answers.

I first encouraged Durah to pray. Praying to a higher power is not like making a list for Santa Claus. It's about opening your heart and letting loving energy seep in, crowding out shame and bitterness. It's surrendering, as Ria did, and releasing the idea of being able to personally control the bad things that come into our lives. It's forming a partnership with a spirit we can't see, hear, or feel in a concrete, material manner; although we can in an emotional, intuitive way. When we feel the spirit, we are no longer alone.

I also encouraged Durah to strengthen her connections with the wonderful women who were at the presentation. The women were of the Christian faith and they sewed and made crafts that helped them financially support themselves and their families. Working together toward common goals and sharing their faith allowed the women to emotionally support each other. I hoped that spiritual and social connections would help give Durah the courage, compassion, and creativity needed to lessen her shame and resentment, and guide her on a liberating, forgiving path forward.

The group of women surrounding Durah worked together to make each other stronger. Craig, a man I met while sitting at a picnic table in the park on a beautiful fall day, was searching for a healing connection.

Craig was a tall, young Native American man who desperately needed dental work, and who appeared to be inebriated as he plunked down beside me with a bag of nachos, two cans of nuts, and a case of beer. "I really need to eat," said Craig as he shoved nachos in his mouth. I had my pen and paper out, writing about forgiveness, which primed me not to fearfully run and hide, but instead listen in case there was a lesson to be learned or a fellow human in need of kindness.

At first, Craig asked to use my phone to call his family and he casually mentioned he needed money. I didn't have money with me and I said I didn't think he should use my phone. But I don't think he sat down beside me because he wanted money or my phone. I think he badly needed to talk and make a human connection.

We chatted about the lovely flowers in the park and the warm sun. He told me he was of the Lakota tribe and I said, "You have an awesome heritage. I know many wonderful people who are Lakota." He complimented me by saying, "You aren't bad for a white woman."

From there Craig told me his brother had just died and he was mad at his mother. He was grieving some family members and feeling hurt by others. He told me life was too hard, and said he wanted to die—that he was suicidal. As with Durah, I wished I could instantly make things better for the young man, but I knew I couldn't. All I could do was try to provide some comfort and support and turn things over to a higher power. We prayed together, and talked about how hard it is to lose people and what we had in common. I praised his honorable career choice of construction work.

When I felt it was time to leave I stood up, and Craig did also. He gave me a big hug and I assured him I would keep praying for him. Then he gave me another hug. His parting words to me were, "We're all the same, aren't we—Lakota and white people?" I agreed and received the gift of a third hug. I hoped our brief, but poignant connection contributed to his courage and helped him keep living and forgiving even though being human is hard.

Forgiveness is a process that is difficult to complete if you feel physically trapped in an abusive or oppressive situation. The situation becomes worse if you are also locked in an internal prison of pain with negative thoughts acting as guards, keeping out any joy, beauty, and love that tries to enter.

The next person you will meet, Lisa, discovered how to forgive when she was safely away from her abusive mother. Like Ria, she also felt spirituality was a key ingredient in her forgiveness journey, but she linked her spirituality to Buddhist philosophy rather than religion and was helped by an excellent therapist.

BREAKING OUT OF OUR PERSONAL PRISONS: LISA'S STORY

Forgiveness is a virtue of the brave.
—INDIRA GANDHI

Lisa was a vivacious, educated, 29-year-old business woman. She grew up in the United States, but her parents were originally from a harsh environment in China. Lisa's mom was severely abused by her father and she, in turn, abused Lisa and her brother. "I grew up having to deal with my mom's constant fits and tantrums," Lisa explained. "They were very violent and at least once a week she would fly into a rage and beat us up really hard. I grew up hating my mom and being afraid a lot. I tried to avoid her rage by being the perfect child, but even little things would tick her off."

Lisa fantasized about her mother going to jail for beating her. She remembered the time she acted on that fantasy. "One time when I was in kindergarten I had gotten beaten up very badly. Even though I was young, I knew what my mom did was wrong, and so I decided I would try to get her caught by exposing to others what she had done to me. I didn't speak English then, so I mooned the class and showed my whole butt, which was full of bloody bruises. The kids started screaming and the teacher freaked out. The teacher grabbed me and brought me into the principal's office. I couldn't decipher what was going on, but I was sent home. My mom then got especially mad and hit me even harder. She said, 'Don't you dare ever do that again.' So after that I kept mum for the longest time. I assumed that no one would actually help me. I started fantasizing about my mom dying early, but felt guilty about thinking that."

Unfortunately, Lisa's cry for help at her school went unanswered and she felt helpless. When we are children our ability to advocate for our own safety and security is limited and adults don't always offer protection.

Things finally changed for Lisa when she was able to move out of her parents' house and attend college. She became aware she could create a new and better life, and she started enjoying more independence and control over her life. Escape from her mother's physical abuse became possible, but there was work to be done mentally and spiritually in order for her to escape self-defeating thoughts and behaviors.

Lisa's first helpful connection was a boyfriend who urged her to seek therapy. She found an effective therapist who used a cognitive-behavioral approach to change the pattern of thinking and behaving that was behind Lisa's difficulties and emotions.

Cognitive-behavioral therapy focuses on challenging and changing detrimental thoughts, beliefs, attitudes and behaviors and developing personal coping strategies. The therapist led Lisa to what she called an "aha moment." But that 'aha' took close to two years of therapy to appear.

Questioning Assumptions and Rewriting Mental Code

Lisa's roadblock was the assumption that her anger was a natural part of her that couldn't be changed. After all, angry fits were what she had observed all her life, and so in her mind they were an inevitable reaction to displeasure.

"I thought angry fits were completely natural in me, and I tried to explain this to the therapist. However, he pushed me and said, 'No, it's not natural. All emotions come from underlying assumptions or beliefs.' He kept urging me to peel back the layers of my anger like an onion. He'd ask me 'What leads you to feel so much anger you want to erupt?' Then he'd ask 'What thought led you to think the thought that led you there?' and then we just kept peeling it back one layer at a time. It was my 'aha' moment when I realized, OMG, you are right—these emotions always come from my underlying thoughts or beliefs. So he made me really question my assumptions, and then things finally clicked."

Lisa felt her dysfunctional upbringing had hampered her maturity. Once she realized she had the ability to understand and change her thinking, she started rapidly improving. "I started really working on changing my assumptions and rewriting the script in my brain. I'm a different person now. I went full in on trying to rewrite my mental code, and I think it's made a huge difference for me."

Rewriting her mental code gave Lisa the prescription she needed to break free of debilitating thoughts and behaviors. Now when she is feeling vulnerable or angry she analyzes and writes down where her feelings are coming from. "When I'm going through a rough time I'll write a note to myself about what I ideally want to be thinking and about things I've achieved—it can be small things like being friendly to someone or completing a task. Then I'll read it to myself. I'm soothing my mind and my feelings by reading the positive thoughts that I've written down. It's like a mantra."

Lisa was often very unforgiving of herself so she found it helpful to step back and consider how others would likely view her. She realized she would never judge her friends as harshly as she was judging herself. Forming a habit of listing things she was proud of each day helped her view herself more positively. She adopted a learning mindset that allowed her to move forward, and she listed things she wanted to improve on as well.

Empathy: The Ability to Understand and Share the Feelings of Another

Empathy is consistently linked to the ability to forgive, and one of the things Lisa wanted to improve on was her ability to empathize. Lisa realized it was hard for her to get out of her own head and understand the feelings of others. "I'm a very headstrong, extremely decisive type of person and tend to question the way other people think."

I asked Lisa if she was able to empathize with her mom. "I don't know if I empathize with her. It seems more like I've just kind of logically understood why she is where she is and decided to be okay with it and let go."

When Lisa was young she observed the way her classmates talked about their moms, and realized they had a very different type of relationship with their mothers than she did. "They loved their moms in a way I have never been able to love my mom. Now I'm respectful of my mom and I can say I love my mom and know that I do, but I love my mom simply because she is my mom. I realize she means well and that she went through worse experiences herself. She didn't get to have an education and was pulled out of school when she was about eleven to work in a factory."

Forgiveness is an ongoing process when it involves relationships that have been hurtful, but that we still choose not to sever. It may be necessary or important to us to find a healthy way to continue a relationship that has caused us pain in the past. "I have a sense of loyalty to family and visit my mom periodically out of a sense of duty," said Lisa. "My mom's not a horrid person. One of the feelings I feel the most is guilt, because I know my mom loves me a lot more than I love her. Could she have done better? Yes. I would have expected her to have learned from what she went through and decided, 'I don't want to put my kids through that.' But she didn't and I accept that's just who she is. I don't know if that's empathy. Perhaps I've just learned to forgive while understanding why she is what she is."

Lisa's mom had never apologized to her and I asked Lisa how she felt about that. She responded, "I guess the way I think of it is that it's pretty pointless to expect an apology. I think that the deepest fault my mom has is that she is not open-minded. She isn't able to listen to criticism in a productive way. She just blocks it off and gets defensive and angry."

"But I see that my mom has tried to improve; for instance, she started reading psychology articles. Now when I come back and visit her she'll say, 'I love you,' which she never did when I was young. She'll try to hold my hand while we're walking. I know she loves me more than I love her. I see this adoration in her eyes, and know she thinks about me and my brother all the time, obsessively, every day. It's like we are her whole world and she makes up a fraction of my world. But I can't get close even though I know that. I guess the forgiveness part of it is I don't really hold anything against her, even if I have trouble really getting close."

Lisa's mom was very proud of her children. They'd had many more opportunities and a much better life than she'd had. Watching her children succeed made Lisa's mom feel successful as well. It also led her to believe that her harsh discipline may have played a beneficial part in her children's achievements. Lisa said, "If anything, my mom feels righteous in what she did and sometimes she likes to say, 'If I wasn't so hard on you, do you think you would be so successful today?' That's something I don't like about her. If she thinks she did something wrong, it shatters her, and so the way she gets past it is to convince herself that what she did was the right thing."

Apologizing requires taking responsibility for pain and hurt we have caused. Becoming aware of the harmful consequences of our past behavior can be a crushing experience. How do people forgive themselves for violently abusing their own children? How do people look back on so many years of their life and conclude they acted horrifically and severely hurt the very people they loved without crumbling into a dark abyss of shame and guilt? Lisa realized her mom (at least for the time being) wasn't strong enough to look at the past with eyes wide open.

A similar dilemma occurred in my own family when my dad was trying to understand why my brother would no longer speak with him. I tried to gently explain how hurt my brother felt by his behaviors. Dad replied, "I've never hurt anyone. Sometimes I've just had to defend myself, that's all." Sometimes, as Jesus said on the cross, we "know not what we do." It takes a lot of strength and courage to accept and take responsibility for our mistakes. Sometimes we just don't have it in us. It's hard to be human.

Conquering Fears and Letting Go

Traumatic family experiences inevitably affect our ability to form and maintain relationships. Lisa's situation with her mother had created feelings of insecurity in her that negatively affected her dating life. She was very fearful of losing a relationship, so she hung on tightly to boyfriends and expected them to fulfill her unmet needs for unconditional love and security. Letting go of unrealistic relationship expectations was difficult.

"I think of forgiveness as letting go, but letting go was the toughest lesson I had to learn. I was obsessed with romance and I was obsessed with being able to claim the love I didn't have. As a result, I had high standards and would put too much weight on a relationship. I quickly became unhappy when my expectations weren't met, mirroring how my mom was always disappointed in me."

"The thing I had to face is, 'How do you let go?' I would just freak out. I couldn't fathom the idea of losing someone. My biggest fear was that the other person would not be able to love me and would quit on me. That fear is something I feel I have actually learned how to deal with very well today. I can have intention and hope and work for something, but without attachment to the result." I asked Lisa how she was able to do that.

"It probably took me a few years of experiences. With each fight, for instance, I used to freak out. I was so afraid that my boyfriend would break up with me. But my freak-outs became less and less intense, and finally I was just done. Now I date with less of that possessiveness and less fear, and I think a lot of that had to do with my weekly therapy sessions. That and reading my books and mantras."

Lisa related the toughest forgiveness experience she had encountered with a boyfriend. "The hardest time I went through was a really bad break-up with a guy I'd dated three and a half years. I thought he was the one, and the relationship was very intense. We had great chemistry but then our love seemed to burst, and a lot of it had to do with his family being super-traditional Indian and unaccepting of me. The breakup happened very suddenly and I was just livid because I had completely opened up my heart, without any defenses. I was just so confident in it that it blindsided me, and I went into a period of deep sadness, grief, and depression for a few months."

Adding Heart Work to the Head Work

But Lisa had been going to therapy and had been working on rewiring her mind. She decided to look at the situation as a challenge instead of a tragedy. "I was badly hurt but I really went full in, and this is when I became even more spiritual. It was like the only thing that could get me out of the pain was spirituality, and so anytime I started feeling weak I would be reading things, writing down mantras. In my room I put up all these pictures that were Zen-like and healing. When I felt afraid I told myself, 'I'm hurting, but I'm going to learn how to let go.' I knew I needed to move on with my life and realized I had a lot to be grateful for. It was a tough challenge, but I'm very proud of how I went through it. Friends who had been with me since college saw a totally different side of me. I turned my pain into productivity."

When negative thoughts have taken you captive, plan an escape and call on the superpower gratitude to come to your rescue. You are not your negative thoughts, but they can kidnap you and keep you from your true self if you're not careful. There's a reason the phrase "count your blessings" is cliché—it works.

Lisa started focusing on the good things in her life and promising opportunities that awaited her. She launched an innovative organization, made new friends, and explored different areas of the city she was living in. The Buddha taught that maintaining good thinking was effortful but worthwhile. Lisa agreed.

"When I was growing up I thought Buddhism was hogwash, but now I've come back to it. I like a lot of the Buddhist teachings and ways of thinking. You can build your life in a very optimistic way, and I'm naturally an optimist. I know there's some luck involved in life, but you do have a lot of control. You can envision your life as you want it to be and be bold enough to go for it. I like to read books by authors like Deepak Chopra and Mark Manson, but to be honest I'm not patient with long books, so I like to read little articles daily and I watch YouTube videos about positive things. I like quotes that are less fluffy and nurturing and more like hard, cold truths, like, 'Hey, wake up! You are your only weakness. This is the way life is, so don't be silly about it.'"

Lisa was a logical person and therapy provided her with logical solutions. But Lisa wasn't able to forgive with her head only; she needed to add some heart. She combined mental exercises with spirituality and formed spiritual habits that created in her a more positive mindset.

I asked Lisa what spirituality meant to her. She said it gave her "mental strength" that allowed her to own her thinking and happiness. She realized she couldn't control the world, but she could control her attitude. "In terms of my spirituality, a lot of it is understanding how complex and vast the universe is. I'm always thinking about that. There's so much out there. I think we're all interconnected and what we do matters. The things you do have implications and affect others. A statement you make could stick with someone and somehow change them and set them on a better path."

Being able to look at the big picture, not just the small snapshot of her personal problems, helped her let go of minor annoyances and expand her heart and mind. "Spirituality helps me take ownership of my life and make the best of it. I believe you can be your greatest friend or enemy. I realize a lot of things we don't forgive are petty, and for me when something is petty I'd rather just move on and let it go. I don't want to be the type of person who's stuck in her own mind, grappling with things and unable to move forward. If you're stuck in your own little prison you are not going to be able to do much good for the rest of the world. There's so much out there. There are people who are suffering worse than you, and you could be applying your energy and heart helping them. There are great issues that humanity is facing today."

"What do you think the relationship is between self and other forgiveness?" I asked Lisa.

"I think it's so important to try to forgive yourself. It's an instinctual thing to be like, 'Oh, My God, I'm so stupid, why did I do that?' and be haunted by regrets and your past, but I think it's important to remember you evolve and are improving, and as long as you know that you are trying your best, what more can you really ask for?"

Peace of mind comes when we are compassionate with ourselves and acknowledge that, as human beings, we will make mistakes and have regrets. Owning up to our flaws and failures can increase our empathy for others as well as make us more humble. Lisa said, "Sometimes I will look at the fact that I have done some stupid shit and I used to be a much worse person—insensitive and clumsy in my social skills, even hurtful of others—and know that I have evolved and become a better person. I apply that to other people and am aware that if time has passed, it is possible that this other person has also changed and improved. I'm always open to that, but also wary. It takes time for someone to really prove themselves to me."

Protect Yourself from Future Harm

Lisa believed it was important to forgive, but also important to protect yourself from future harm. "Sometimes you have to let go of people that you determine are not good for you. If the person made a big mistake and really owns up to it, however, it's worth giving them another chance. Time will tell."

Bad feelings can easily reappear when we're faced with a person or situation from the past that we associate with danger of some kind. Our fear response will be activated to protect us from harm. We can't always avoid people who may want to shame, disrespect, or abuse us, so it's good to prepare ourselves for tough situations that could make their way into our futures. Our fear of vulnerability lessens when we are equipped with connections, courage, compassion, and creativity.

Lisa worked diligently to escape her personal prison and became empowered through forgiveness. However, we sometimes hang on to our victim identities and hold tight to grudges. Why?

Victim status may bring benefits in terms of attention, sympathy, feelings of superiority, and compensation. We may become locked into our identity as a sufferer and comfortable with our discomfort. Changing paths may seem daunting and perhaps we can't imagine how to travel to a new, more joyful, liberating destination.

Lisa learned how to protect herself so she could move forward without unnecessary fear. You can too. We can be survivors and heroes. Forgiveness can empower us and lead us to a better place and an identity we can be proud of.

Breaking out of our personal prisons requires courage such as shown by Lisa. But being human is hard and before we break free we may need to enter what our next forgiveness hero, Esther, called the House of Sorrows.

Gather Courage to Confront Difficult Situations and Emotions

Emotional pain is not something that should be hidden away and never spoken about. There is truth in your pain, there is growth in your pain, but only if it's first brought out into the open.
—STEVEN AITCHISON

When we've been badly hurt, is it okay to cry, grieve, and enter what Anne of Green Gables called "the depths of despair?" I hope you said yes, because grieving time is often a necessary part of healing time. When we grieve we enter what Esther, our next forgiveness hero, referred to as the House of Sorrows. The House of Sorrows is a temporary dwelling, like a shelter from the storm. While there, we confront our pain, our fears, our disappointment, and our shame. We grieve for our lost dreams and unmet expectations. But we don't want to remain in the House of Sorrows too long because our purpose is not to become hopeless victims of adversity. We enter the House of Sorrows with the purpose of uncovering and processing our pain. We weather the storm and emerge ready to move forward with courage, compassion, and creativity.

American culture emphasizes individualism and emotional strength. We may be urged to "just get over it" when we are hurting from a painful event. It's embarrassing to admit our true feelings and so we apologize for our tears and for showing what we believe is emotional weakness. But in truth our tears can lead us to emotional awareness, healing, and strength.

The term *emotional* has been linked to showing sadness and sentimentality and is generally regarded as soft and weak, while showing anger, which is certainly an emotion, is often linked with strength. However, does it take strength to be angry, or is it just a natural reaction when things don't go our way? Is it weak to admit we're sad and hurting, or are we showing courage when we uncover our pain?

Anger may be linked with strength because it can be risky to show anger unless you are in a power position. Yell at your boss and you will probably get fired. The boss yells at you and you do what he or she wants.

All of us humans feel anger and sadness, whether we express it or not. We may try to avoid the House of Sorrows and our true feelings, but they will undoubtedly find a way to haunt us. If we try to bury our sorrow, it will keep bursting forth, perhaps manifesting itself in physical illness, temper tantrums, headaches, or depression. There's a reason we can't get something out of our mind, and uncovering that reason is a key to unleashing it and letting it go.

ENTERING THE HOUSE OF SORROWS: ESTHER'S STORY

THE GUEST HOUSE
—BY RUMI

This being human is a guest house.
Every morning a new arrival.

A joy, a depression, a meanness,
some momentary awareness comes
as an unexpected visitor.

Welcome and entertain them all!
Even if they are a crowd of sorrows,
who violently sweep your house
empty of its furniture,
still, treat each guest honorably.

He may be clearing you out
for some new delight.

The dark thought, the shame, the malice.
Meet them at the door laughing and invite them in.

Be grateful for whoever comes.
Because each has been sent
as a guide from beyond.

Our next story is of Esther, a 72-year-old woman who wasn't afraid of the House of Sorrows and who was able to courageously burst the bubble of her rage and resentment. Esther had lived in Turkey and Canada as well as the United States, and was well traveled. She shared her story with me in a Lutheran church, but she loved learning from many different wisdom traditions, including Sufism, Buddhism, Lakota spirituality, Catholicism, and ancestral traditions. Reading about spirituality and religion was a favorite pastime of Esther, and forgiveness was something she had been continually practicing.

Esther related to me one of her first empowerment experiences with forgiveness. Her story involved forgiving a coworker who had been disrespecting her in front of others. She was able to let go of the rage and bitterness inside her by having the courage to stand up to her offender.

Esther explained, "I had been working in the construction field for five years, and was involved in doing electrical wiring. My first construction job was on a team with thirteen people and seven of us were women. After that I worked with an individual man. My next job was with a crew that was preparing a barn for a hundred people to live in and do spiritual and self-discovery work. I was excited because I had never worked with a crew of, supposedly, seekers or people who were spiritually savvy before. Unfortunately, I found the crew's prejudice toward women in construction absolutely numbing. I had a lot of anger, I mean, really rage."

Esther was especially angry and disappointed because she had expected the crew to be reasonable. She thought everyone would work together and support each other since they all shared a spiritual mission. But that didn't happen. "We needed to build a trench for an armored cable and we needed to do it through solid rock. I was there with almost 40 men and I was being trashed on all the time. It was bad. What I found was narrowness, prejudice, and unacceptable behavior. I was very bitter. I had a lot of rage, daily."

How did Esther let go of her rage? She began by realizing that if she wanted to move forward and get her work done she needed space to process what was happening to her. It helped to have a physical job, she explained, because that helped her get rid of some of her unproductive anger energy. But she also needed to step back and observe the men, the way they were with each other and the way they were with her. The men were trying to control her in big ways, such as not helping her with work tasks, and small ways, such as telling her she couldn't take a shower in the morning. She realized she needed the courage to stand up for herself.

"I didn't really crack this nut of forgiveness until one day, we were working on what's called a double, and I was working on a platform above the men. We had a very limited number of extension cords, and one of the men demanded that I give him my cord because 'the men needed to work.' I said, 'I'm working up here too,' and 'I'm not going to do it.' They said, 'Well, ra ra ra ra ra,' so I just cut the cord. For some reason, that explosion and standing up for myself really popped the bubble of my anger and I made a boundary. I did it publicly, in the heat of the moment, while everybody was watching. It helped that I was physically so far above them. I was safe. I was protected. I was in control. From then on, a whole other pattern opened up. I got quite a reputation and a lot of respect before the job was over."

Sometimes, however, we feel guilty about standing up for ourselves. Are we being selfish? Maybe we're wrong to speak out? Should we be holding our anger in instead of letting it out? Women especially are often socialized to be accommodating and compliant, not confrontational. But holding in rage against abuse is like receiving a daily dose of poison. The effect will be toxic and, left untreated, disastrous.

Esther felt conflicted about her bold actions and believed she needed forgiveness for what many of us would call appropriate assertive behavior. "I acted wickedly that day," said Esther.

"Really I did. But I also thought, 'I don't care what any of them say about me, or what any of them do. I needed to do what I did and I'm going to forgive myself for doing it.'"

Setting Boundaries, Releasing Fear, Expanding Awareness

"How did your experience help you forgive your offenders?" I asked.

"Once I set my boundaries and felt safe I experienced an expanding of space. I started being able to see more deeply into my offender's situation and I could better understand him. Releasing my fears allowed me to open up and have compassion. Forgiveness means realizing that the people you need to forgive aren't bigger, or stronger, or more powerful than you are. It's very likely that they are weaker; that they are coming from a place of fear or ignorance. Once the person is no longer on a pedestal, you can see the person as an equal and you can stand up for yourself and make the necessary boundaries. It's an expanded feeling of heart."

When Esther's anger exploded and she regained her self-respect, she could start looking at her offender as a person, not just a hurtful, oppressive object. She could start empathizing with him. Forgiveness didn't happen all at once; it was a process. "I think the resolution took place within three or four months. I remember we had talks after my explosion and I got to know him better. We'd talk while waiting for dinner and I found out quite a lot about him. He was from Alaska and had been a longshoreman. He'd had to work on jobs that were very tough both physically and mentally. We resolved our conflict to the point where I was able to think of him fondly."

When Esther popped the bubble of her anger, she had issues to resolve not just with her main offender, but also with the other men who were struggling with their biases toward women in construction. "My conflict with the other men escalated at that point. So I made a series of decisions that established boundaries and let the men know that's just the way it was going to be. I didn't care what they thought of me, what they said about me, and what they said to other people about me. I was a woman on a mission and I could clearly see my purpose. The rest of it really didn't matter."

Humility Empowers Forgiveness

Esther's courage and strength allowed her to become more compassionate and forgiving of human frailties. "There was a softening that took place," Esther explained. "I understood that I could be offensive too, and that it isn't their problem and it's not my problem. It's the human condition."

Role models help us learn how to deal with our anger and bitterness. The leader of the project Esther was working on was an inspiration to her. "I learned so much about humility and humiliation during that period of time. I would be so angry at those stupid men and their filthy ways of being in the world, and then I saw our leader who was humble, who was humiliated over and over again, but who did not go into reaction. He would state his case and quietly walk away. And I really wanted to be like that—more than anything else."

Esther worked on her ability to keep calm and observe a situation before reacting. She related the story of a friend whom she knows is weak and fearful. "My friend is weaker than me and gets frightened easily when she doesn't understand things. Then she lashes out at me, but I can let that go right through me like the wind and not react negatively. It's important for my friend and others in our group to see the entrance of light in a dark situation."

Esther felt that people in the United States aren't very good at facing hurt and disappointment. "I've traveled many places and it seems that in America, we will do anything to deny or avoid pain. We don't want to take ownership or responsibility for our pain. We go through blaming and shaming until we may finally realize that maybe, just maybe, this has a little bit to do with me."

"How did you have the courage to take responsibility?" I asked Esther.

"I accepted that we, as human beings, don't treat each other well. We can all be violent, unresponsive, selfish. It's our human nature. We're all a part of the mess. So as a human being, I have to forgive myself all the time."

"How are self-forgiveness and forgiveness of others related?" I inquired.

"Forgiveness of self has to come before forgiveness of others. You can say, 'I forgive you' to someone, but it won't be genuine until you've looked inside, you've seen who you are, and you've forgiven. You scrub yourself clean and it's only then that you can view others with compassion and forgive."

I probed further. "How can we feel loved and scrubbed clean when we're so aware of the awful things we've done and the hurtful things that have shamed us?"

"That's where faith comes in. Forgiveness is God's gift to suffering humanity. Forgiveness transforms us. Four or five times I've felt like I've been rebuilt, cell by cell, from the inside out. The Divine Spirit has reached down and said, 'Well, we're just going to have to rebuild you.' And I got healthy, grounded, balanced, and new. I became a new person."

Wounded Healers

Esther's faith was essential to her forgiveness experience, but she also emphasized the importance of being aided by wounded healers and becoming one herself. I asked her who a wounded healer was. "Wounded healers walk with people who are in pain and they listen without judgment or advice. They show compassion and they are able to calmly observe and reflect instead of react. That's hard to do."

"What makes forgiveness hard for you?" I asked.

"I'm doing pretty well with fear and am sometimes even amazed by my courage. But pride comes up all the time. The Benedictine Spirituality advises that we pray every day that we are humiliated. That way we have to keep working on controlling excessive pride and developing compassion."

Esther found the courage to confront her sorrows through spiritual and social connections. She obtained wisdom through various religious and philosophical sources, and was able to view adversity with gratitude.

Once we've uncovered our pain and can better understand it, it's time to have the courage to move on. Our next forgiveness hero, Katherine, had to work very hard to uncover repressed anger towards her mother. She was guided by a therapist and supported by her Christian faith. Confronting her buried sorrow was scary and effortful, but well worth the joy and freedom she felt when she could finally let go of the hurt that had blocked her healing.

LEAVING THE HOUSE OF SORROWS: KATHERINE'S STORY

Forgiving is not forgetting.
Forgiving is remembering without pain.
—CELIA CRUZ

Katherine was a 76-year-old Christian woman who had attended both Catholic and Protestant churches. Forgiveness was not a stranger to her, but none of her past experiences were as transformative as the one that occurred about three years before our interview. She, like Ria, had thought she'd forgiven, but discovered she had actually been repressing hurt and shame that she had not been able to confront. When she gained the courage to uncover her pain and grieve, healing began.

Katherine's journey of discovery began when her husband, whom she'd loved and cared for in their home with the help of hospice, passed away. "My problem was not the grief I felt, but the grief I could *not* feel. There was something I couldn't get at.

So after my husband died, I attended a grief class and individual counseling sessions. I'm a believer in counseling because I've had a lot of occasions in my life when I have benefitted from it.

"I talked to the grief counselor, who was also the person who led the group class, and I said, 'I can't cry. I can't grieve over my deceased husband. There's something wrong with that, I don't like it.' I've never been a big person with tears anyway. I have very deep emotions, but I don't display them easily. I told the counselor, 'This really bothers me. There's something not quite right, but I don't know what it is.'"

An internal struggle was taking place in Katherine that she did not understand. Something in her subconscious was yearning to break free, but was conflicted about how to do so. Neuropsychologists have identified a part of our brain called the 'executive function' that collects information and gets to be the decider for us on a conscious level. It receives signals and messages from other parts of our mind. The fear*ful* part of Katherine's subconscious was determined to keep buried frightening parts of her past that the fear*less* part of her was trying to unleash. The courageous part of her mind was not giving up, however, and found a sneaky way to help free her of repressed toxic thoughts and feelings.

One day Katherine walked into her counselor's office wearing a totally different outfit than she would normally wear. She usually dressed in a very traditional and classic manner, but that day she wore a frilly skirt and top.

"Do you notice anything about the way I am dressed?" Katherine asked her counselor.

"Tell me about that," replied the counselor.

"Well, I don't know … I'm not sure what's going on inside me."

The counselor probed, "What's different about what you're wearing?"

"I'm wearing a skirt."

"Why is that unusual?"

"Because my mother always wore skirts, and I haven't wanted to be like her."

The grief counselor kept searching for answers with other questions, but that day Katherine was still too scared to fully uncover what was bothering her. However, what the counselor said next frightened Katherine even more.

"You know what is bothering you, but it's buried so deep that perhaps I need to refer you to a therapist who can better help you."

Katherine explained why that statement frightened her. "That scared me because I was very comfortable with my counselor. I felt like I could say anything to her. So I thought, 'I have to get this out. I don't want to go to someone else.' On the way home from our session, I was able to pinpoint it. It was there—just ready to come up, but I didn't know how to get it out. I emailed my counselor and said, 'I think I know what it is. I think I'm very angry with my mother and I'm holding it all in. I've been holding it in forever and ever and ever, and this is preventing me from grieving and having the emotions that are probably normal.'"

Uncovering and Releasing Pain

The counselor suggested Katherine write her thoughts down and bring them to their next session, which she did. Katherine explained. "We talked about what I'd written for a while and then everything just started spilling out—all the anger I'd been holding in. Everything started bubbling up. My counselor said, 'You're holding on to so much anger that you can't grieve for your deceased husband,' and then we talked about forgiveness and that became the focus. I thought I'd forgiven my mother because I had examined certain issues but, in truth, I was still holding on to a lot of unforgiveness. What my mother did hurt me terribly. Maybe it wouldn't have hurt others as much, but because of the person I was, it was extremely painful. My counselor said, 'We have some work to do.'"

Katherine set out to do that work and had a long talk with her brother and sister-in-law during a 400-mile drive to visit relatives. She wondered if her brother had feelings about their mother similar to her own. In Katherine's family mothers raised girls and fathers raised boys, so she knew her brother's interactions with their mother were much more limited than hers.

Katherine told her story during the drive and her brother reflected, "I didn't realize all that was going on with you. I had no idea." Her sister-in-law was a good listener and an open person who made a statement during the trip that heavily impacted Katherine. She said, "I think you made excuses for your mom, but you've never forgiven her."

What's the difference between excusing someone and forgiving them? Excusing means we have come up with reasons why our offender did something and have decided those reasons were legitimate. In Katherine's case, she knew her mother had grown up in an orphanage and didn't have an opportunity to learn parenting outside of an institutional setting. Katherine could rationally understand why her mother unknowingly made parenting judgments that hurt her. But forgiveness involves both the heart and the head. Deep inside, the young girl who struggled and hurt so badly as a result of her mother's parenting was still ashamed and angry. Katherine had not yet made peace with a painful and confusing time period in her life.

"What was it about your relationship with your mother that hurt you so profoundly you couldn't confront it for almost sixty years?" I asked.

"I felt very, very strongly that my mother robbed me of my teenage years. I loved being around friends, but my mother grew up in an orphanage and didn't understand how boys and girls interact. When I was around twelve or thirteen, I went over to a friend's house and we were playing some games like spin the bottle but were doing nothing bad. However, my mom heard about it from someone and from that point on she wouldn't let me go out with my friends. She robbed me of my friends and I felt isolated."

"Since I couldn't be with my friends, my friendships couldn't be sustained. I'd always been an outgoing person and had friends in school, but all of a sudden that was gone and I felt so alone.

It may not have been a big deal for someone else but for me it was huge, absolutely huge. I was part of a big family, but I still felt extremely alone. I started comforting myself by eating. I became very obese."

Katherine's mother felt she was protecting her by limiting social interactions, but the consequences were not safety and security, but horrible pain and loneliness. "I had no one to talk to," Katherine remembered, "because my mother had basically ousted me from my friends. I couldn't talk to my mother because she would put up an iron curtain. I couldn't talk to my dad because he raised the boys. I had this terrible feeling of isolation."

Being isolated from friends during her teenage years affected Katherine's social development. "I didn't know how to act around other women or men as I grew up because I didn't have the opportunities and experiences that would have helped me learn how to interact. I went to an all-girls school and the other girls got to go out, but I was socially isolated during my formative years when I was trying to find my identity. It took me years to catch up."

Genuine, emotional forgiveness means understanding not only our offender, but also understanding the impact the offense had on us. Often there is shame and embarrassment we have to face, along with the anger we feel towards the person we are blaming for our shame and embarrassment. Because our offender's actions led to experiences in our lives we regret, self-compassion and self-forgiveness becomes a component of the process of letting go.

Why was the pain that occurred in Katherine's relationship with her mother buried so very deep and why was it so difficult to uncover? In our youth, we have few resources to deal with painful situations. If we can find no way to productively handle a difficult situation, we may deny, repress, and displace our hurt. Katherine experienced isolation and loneliness during a developmental period that is essential to social learning and identity formation. She had no one to provide the guidance and support she needed during her teenage years, so she experienced terrible hurt and confusion that led to deep-seated unforgiveness. Her pain became buried because she did not know how to process it.

A part of Katherine realized it was time to get rid of the burden that was blocking her genuine emotions from being released. She told her counselor, "I really need to do some work on this."

The counselor responded, "Did you ever talk to your mother about your feelings?"

"No, she was the kind of person who would deny or gloss over things. She'd change the subject and wouldn't talk about anything she really didn't want to talk about. So I was afraid of crossing her. My younger sisters defied her and got into real trouble. They ended up being sent away to boarding school."

Katherine could not talk to her mother as a teenager because she feared her, and in later years she was unable to share her hurt because she perceived that her mother, like Lisa's, would not have been strong enough to confront the consequences of her actions and so would have simply denied her part in the pain or acted defensively by shifting responsibility. Katherine felt her mother's denial and defensiveness would only make her feel worse.

Katherine's father went along with her mother because of the disciplinary boundaries that had been set. She had little access to her dad and felt he didn't love her. Later on she realized he did, but just didn't know how to show it.

The counselor replied, "You didn't have a chance to talk to your mother openly and honestly when she was alive, but you can go ahead and write her a letter now. Tell her how you feel."

Katherine followed her counselor's advice. "I started spewing out why I was angry, and I was feeling pretty angry. I thought, 'This is the work I need to do.' I thought about it and thought about it and contemplated and reflected. I talked to my counselor and then wrote the letter. I'll never forget the feeling I had. I sat out at a park on a bench with some paper and I just started writing. As I started writing, I felt as if I was speaking to my mother and the tears just poured out. I had some friends walk by and they asked me if I was okay. I said, 'I'm fine, I'm just doing some work I need to do.'"

Katherine's counselor advised her that she could do what she wanted with the letter—tear it up, burn it, leave it somewhere, whatever. The important thing was that she completed the letter.

"I went home and walked out to my garden. I love my garden. I love being outside. I burned the letter in my garden. I sent it out, and for me that was symbolic because the earth and the garden are very real for me. I felt in touch with the different elements."

Liberation

A hurt as deep as Katherine's doesn't disappear instantly, but her actions propelled her healing. "I didn't feel better immediately, but I started being able to cry and I would get emotional going to a movie. I would talk to people about very deep things and could actually feel myself tear up and would think, 'My goodness, this is very unusual, I'm not used to this.' But I knew that the words to my mother had been sent and I had done the forgiveness because I no longer felt I was pushing my feelings down. I was able to let go of my pain, and oh, it has transformed my life in a way that is really hard to describe. I've done other forgiveness things, but this one was just so huge. It was at the bottom, in a pit. So it was the deepness of it."

Katherine started thinking of her mother differently. "Previous to forgiveness, I could never say nice things about my mother. Now I'm softer towards her and can say she was a very beautiful, smart woman and was a wonderful cook. Now that I've forgiven my mother for what impacted me so hard and have accepted the way she was, I can also say that I love to cook. I no longer feel hatred toward her, and so it's okay to be like her. It took me over sixty years, but maybe that's why I feel so joyful and content."

Katherine's experience made her aware of the emotional roadblocks that can stand in the way of joy and peace of mind. She loved the feeling of freedom that came from unleashing buried anger and pain. "Now I can tear up and cry. It doesn't bother me. It's not like I have to hold anything down. It's just been so liberating—that's the only word I can use for it."

It can be hard to truly understand our emotions or realize when we may be repressing or avoiding an issue that needs uncovering. Because Katherine realized the joy that comes with forgiveness she often prayed, "Lord, if there's some unforgiveness in me that I don't recognize or I have pushed down, I want you to make it clear to me when the time is right for me and the other person, whether they're living or dead."

Courage to Be Vulnerable

Katherine started wondering if her inability to be emotional in the past had affected her children. Now that she wasn't fearful of her genuine feelings she wanted to be more open with them. She thought, "Is there something that happened that I did, because of my manner, because of not being able to show my emotions, that I need to confront to help my family forgive?"

Katherine's son was going to a counselor, so she volunteered to attend a session and answer any questions that might help her son progress. "I just answered as honestly as I could and that felt so good. When asked questions before, I would have fudged a bit because I wasn't open enough and willing to admit mistakes. I might have unknowingly kept secret certain things that would have been the heart of what he needed to hear. I wouldn't have been able to get to the real stuff—the mending part. I wouldn't have been able to see the whole story from his viewpoint because

I would have been too busy protecting my ego. I focused on what he needed to know and remembered it was not about me."

Katherine now realizes the importance of meeting unfinished business head on. "I'm always praying for the courage and strength to face forgiveness issues because I know that even though it's scary, I will feel so liberated, relieved, and joyful to have been a part of something that is healing."

I asked Katherine to explain further her spirituality. "I have a whole world within myself. I have a strong connection to God and feel that God is within me. I think we are not meant to operate on our own."

Unconditional Love

Katherine talked about how her dreams for the future had been affected by her forgiveness work. While putting together a collage with some young children, she was drawn to pictures of happy families. She also became focused on the picture of a flame. Those visual images stimulated her thinking and she reflected on what they meant to her. "I discovered that I wanted to be a flame. A flame—a light—a ray of sunshine that could give my family and others unconditional love."

"How is unconditional love related to forgiveness?" I asked.

"I can't do one without the other. It takes all the depths of your soul to love someone or others unconditionally because they are obviously going to do some things you do not like. Unconditional love doesn't mean making excuses for someone, it means loving them even when they act in ways of which you don't approve."

Katherine noted that her mother never learned how to give unconditional love. "My mother didn't have unconditional love to give. Her love was based on whether you did the right thing or not, and if not you got sent away."

Katherine realized that her second husband, to whom she was married for 26 years and for whom she had cared for until he died, had given her unconditional love. Katherine had certainly loved her husband, but during their years together she was still learning how forgiveness and unconditional love worked. "Until I could forgive my mother and make peace with a painful period of my life, how could I give myself fully to someone else? I was holding back and unconditional love is everything about not holding back."

Katherine was able to be the flame and the light of unconditional love when she took her granddaughter on a big trip to Africa. Her granddaughter, who struggled with certain issues, didn't always behave appropriately and during the trip became good at pushing Grandma's buttons. When that happened Katherine let her know what behavior she didn't like, but she also reassured her of her love. She told her, "I just want to let you know that I love you unconditionally. I may not like the things you do and they may bother me, but it's never going to take away how I feel about you as a person. I will always love you."

Her granddaughter responded, "Wow, Grandma, I heard that there was such a thing, but I didn't understand it."

Katherine explained that she works at viewing the difficult people in her life with compassion, instead of just seeing them as objects inflicting pain. "I don't want to feel the pain that comes if I can't forgive someone for just being who they are, even though I don't agree with or like what they're doing. It's about accepting them wherever they're at in life. I can hope they change, but they may not and I just need to love them through it. I try to look at people with compassion and I often realize they must be hurting terribly inside. When I see that, I can't be angry."

Compassionate Heart and Open Mind

"How are you able to look at people who hurt you with compassion?" I inquired.

"One thing I do is pray. That calms me and helps me be more objective. Instead of wishing for revenge, I pray that people are happy and able to overcome whatever demons they may be facing. I try to look at the people I'm angry with like God would, and I become softer toward them. I give my problems up to God, and know that he is with me and knows better than I do. Relying on God takes a lot of the burden off."

I asked Katherine what she felt her greatest impediment to forgiveness was. She responded, "Thinking I'm better than other people. Where did I get that idea? Probably from my insecurity. To overcome my lack of confidence, I needed to perceive myself as better than the people I felt were judging me. So I have to correct myself a lot and face my own faults. I have to take a second look at a situation and say 'Okay, you're creating your own stumbling blocks.'"

Forgiveness is hampered when we think we're better than others or when we think we're worse. Accepting ourselves and others as we are is not easy. We tend to believe we or the people we are upset with should know better. We judge without mercy, which blocks understanding. It takes courage to ask questions like, "Why do they perceive this matter differently than me?" "What could I do to help us communicate better? How can I improve this situation?" But accepting differences and working towards understanding facilitates forgiveness.

Katherine described one of the benefits of forgiveness as having the courage to be your real self. "Other people can put on airs or criticize, but that doesn't bother you because you are who you are. You've gotten over the hurdle, so you can be yourself and not worry about what other people think of you. When you're in that pain of unforgiveness you are always putting on some kind of show. You don't realize it, but you are, and so you're not being real. You can't interact with other people in a genuine, sincere fashion. You don't intend to be superficial—it's just that you have blockages to figure out."

I asked Katherine what she thought the relationship was between self-forgiveness and forgiveness of others. "The Golden Rule states, 'Do onto others as you would have them do onto you.' If you can't forgive yourself or treat yourself with compassion, you won't be able to do that for others. You can be more open to forgiving others when you forgive yourself because you can think, 'If I was doing this or that wrong, maybe they're in a similar position. Or maybe they have other tough things going on.' So you look at people in a different way. They are no longer objects hurting you or causing you to make bad decisions. You're more objective."

Forgiveness Sets Us Free

A sense of humor is a sign that we've let go of our pride and shame and felt the relief that letting go brings through laughter. Katherine had found laughter to be great medicine and an indication that she had let go of whatever she was struggling with. "We're human and we suffer from the human condition. If we can laugh at ourselves instead of beating ourselves up, we free ourselves from fear and defensiveness. The barriers come down and we can reach out for help."

"What advice would you give others regarding forgiveness?" I asked.

"If you have ghosts or struggles that can be rectified by forgiveness, I'd say run toward it. Don't be afraid of anything because forgiveness will set you free. Forget that there might be a little pain attached to it. Embrace it, embrace it. Embrace it because it's just so freeing."

It takes courage for us to enter the house of sorrows and it takes courage for us to leave it. Katherine needed to grieve for the mother and childhood she had wanted but never had. She confronted her past anger, embarrassment, loneliness, and confusion. She then worked to understand her painful experience and remember it in a new light. She was able to leave the house of sorrows with a positive attitude and the courage needed to create a life filled with joy, unconditional love, freedom, and openness.

Forgiveness requires courage because to genuinely and deeply forgive, we must get in touch with our inner demon. Our inner demon is actually well intentioned. It's simply trying to help us survive and defend us from those who may hurt us, but in the process of doing so it often prevents us from finding the joy and freedom that comes from letting go of fear, loving, and forgiving.

The next chapter will focus on our struggle to attain the virtue of humility, which has been called the master virtue because of its ability to help us with other virtues.

HUMILITY: ARE YOU IN TOUCH WITH YOUR INNER DEMON?

Courage is what it takes to stand up and speak;
courage is also what it takes to sit down and listen.
—WINSTON CHURCHILL

In my earlier years, I would not have associated humility with courage—and for good reason. The dictionary definition of humility is a modest or low view of one's own importance, with synonyms being meekness, unassertiveness, diffidence, submissiveness. It didn't seem to me that it took much courage to be meek and modest. I didn't need to try hard or gather strength to NOT assert myself or to submissively go along with the crowd.

But spiritual humility is not about cowardice, although it may appear that way to someone who has learned to be impressed with the loud, aggressive, and forceful behavior our society tends to applaud. It's about courage and discerning, as Winston

Churchill noted, when we need to stand up and speak and when we need to sit down and listen.

The definition of humility that is associated with courage and forgiveness is: the ability to clearly perceive, and the willingness to accept, one's strengths and weaknesses.[21] Spiritually, it means recognizing there is a power greater than ourselves whom we can trust to love and guide us.[22] It isn't easy to truthfully perceive our strengths and weaknesses, accept ourselves in all our grand imperfection, and have faith in a spiritual source we can sense but not touch. Those abilities, however, help us gain the courage to forgive.

The Japanese have a word, *wabi-sabi*, which means finding beauty in imperfection and impermanence. Embracing imperfection and celebrating our ability to learn and grow creates a more joyful life—a forgiving life.

The people I interviewed found forgiveness challenging for various reasons. Some felt ashamed and embarrassed by what had happened to them and struggled with feelings of inferiority. In other cases, forgiveness was difficult because excessive pride and arrogance kept them from viewing an offender with compassion. My forgiveness heroes were able to forgive when they balanced feelings of inferiority and superiority and were able to see their offenders as neither better nor worse than themselves. After several interviews, I started conceptualizing humility as a self-confidence continuum and constructed the following table.

Effect of the Humility Continuum on Forgiveness		
Feelings of Inferiority	HUMILITY	Feelings of Superiority
Fear of Confrontation	Courage to Confront Fears	Fear of Losing Status/Power
Avoidance, Repression	Acceptance, Compassion	Revenge, Aggression
Self-Blame, Shame	Forgiveness	Blame Others, Arrogance

Sometimes fear of confrontation with those we consider more powerful or worthy blocks forgiveness because we repress or hide our true feelings. Sometimes fear of losing status or power prevents us from forgiving because we want to maintain the status quo and are not open to differing perspectives. We may feel both at the same time or go back and forth between feelings of inferiority and superiority, which is why I included arrows going both ways.

When we are powerless or perceive ourselves as powerless, others may be in a position to offend and abuse us. Children are especially vulnerable because of their dependence on adults and because they are only beginning to learn skills that will strengthen and support them through tough times. As adults, we acquire more independence, but may have what psychologists call "learned helplessness." Learned helplessness refers to a sense of powerlessness that arises from past trauma or repeated failures. We lose our hope and motivation because we lack the courage, knowledge, or ability necessary to overcome our shame through self-compassion and creating healthier thought and behavior patterns.

If feelings of powerlessness are causing our shame and resentment, having the courage to stand up for ourselves and take responsibility and ownership of a situation may be the spark needed to ignite forgiveness. If I keep quiet and try to overlook or forget about offensive behavior, I am likely to sizzle and seethe inside. I may fear confronting my offender at the same time I am cringing with shame at that fear. My dismay may cause me to direct my bitterness either inside at myself or outside at an object of blame.

When we realize our strength and conquer our fears, offenders no longer have power over us. Offenders are no longer objects of hurt and injustice, but fellow human beings doing the best they can, given the point they have reached on their life's journey. Our vision is no longer blocked by pain and defensiveness, so we can look at others with eyes of compassion and empathy and see them, and ourselves, more clearly.

When we are feeling inferior and fear confrontation, we typically will not have the courage to become forgiveness heroes. At the opposite end, when we feel superior and are afraid of losing status or power, we also will likely not have the courage to be forgiveness heroes. We puff up with pride and enjoy feeling better than others we have decided are less moral or righteous than us. It's nice to feel that we are champions of goodness, doing our part to punish or destroy the bad people. Or at least tell them off and put them in their place; perhaps smugly advising them they will go to hell or some other dark place where demons dwell.

We may create a wall of moral superiority that protects our egos from damage.

Unfortunately demons dwell in our minds and they attempt to influence us when they tell us things like "You're better than that person," or "Those people are evil." I believe there are evil actions and that there are behaviors that are better than others. I also believe we are more likely to commit those evil actions and behaviors when we believe we are better than others and when we believe a certain group of people are evil.

The Dangers of Labeling People as Good or Bad

What's so bad about labeling people good or bad? If we believe someone is wholly evil, there is no reason to listen to the inferior being. Why hear the stories or try to understand the perspectives of people we know are wicked and dangerous? They should simply be punished or eliminated, and certainly not forgiven—unless perhaps they submit to whatever it is we, as superior beings, require of them. Slavery and oppression have been very popular in human history because of that trend in our thinking.

It takes a lot of courage to confront our inner demons and realize that, in certain circumstances, we too may be capable of the very evil we despise. Our fear is that we are as "bad" as those we have judged negatively. We tell ourselves, "I would *never* do something like that." But strength lies in asking ourselves, "Could I do something like that?" The next question to ask ourselves is, "How can I prevent myself from doing something like that?"

Elias Chacour, a Palestinian Christian, in his book *Blood Brothers: The Dramatic Story of a Palestinian Christian Working for Peace in Israel,* wrote about his struggle with forgiveness.

> *Silent, still, I lay there, aware for the first time that I was capable of vicious, killing hatred. Aware that all men everywhere--despite the thin, polite veneer of society—are capable of hideous violence against other men. Not just the Nazis or the Zionists or the Palestinian commandos—but me. I had covered my hurts with Christian responses, but inside the anger had gnawed. With this sudden, startling view of myself, a familiar inner voice spoke firmly, without compromise: If you hate your brother, you are guilty of murder. Now I understood.* (Chacour & Hazard, 2013, p. 171.)

Recognition of the need for forgiveness and the capacity for goodness and evil in all human beings can lead to diminution of anger and greater calm. It signals acceptance of our human nature. That acceptance breaks down a wall and allows us to communicate with others more effectively. We reach a deeper understanding and grow spiritually.

When I taught world history, I was careful when explaining violent, destructive events like the Holocaust. It's instinctive to demonize those who hurt our group and idolize those who defend our group. My worry was that I would unintentionally contribute to more hatred and violence in the world by creating future warriors who would find purpose in seeking revenge or doing battle with the "bad" people. I wanted to create understanding and awareness of different perspectives, not stereotypes or simplistic good guys versus bad guys thinking. Nations are made of people and therefore have strengths and weaknesses, just as people do.

Don't Let Your Inner Demons Trick You

The good news is that if we understand and are in touch with our inner demon, we take away the demon's power. We know what our inner demons are up to and how they are trying to scare us. The Lakota Indian culture has teaching stories illustrating how easy it is for us to be deceived by negative inner voices that are personified by the trickster character *Iktomi*. I like the idea of a trickster influencing us because it directs us to think about what is going on in our minds so we can avoid being led astray.

It's also helpful to remember the biology of our brains. The inner demon can be depicted as our brain's limbic system, which contains our amygdala, a part of the brain that directs our survival instincts. When my sometimes overprotective amygdala is sending me fearful survival messages, I can upshift my thinking to the cerebral cortex, the center for higher brain functions and deep thinking. If I'm able to pause after an offense occurs, I can exert self-control and reflect, instead of reacting without mindful thought. There's a biological reason for the "count to ten" advice.

It's natural to become angry and sad, afraid and defensive when things don't go our way and when we do not fully understand what is happening to us. We have to grapple with our dark side and seek the light. Yoda from Star Wars said: *In a dark place we find ourselves, and a little more knowledge lights our way.*

Forgiveness can get complicated. For example, I may be afraid to confront my boss and so I avoid dealing with an issue, but at the same time, I feel my boss is less intelligent and talented than I am and blame her for a problem at my job. Humility gives me the courage to talk with my boss about the problems I perceive. I can be assertive, not aggressive, in voicing my concerns. Humility gives me the courage to take responsibility for whatever is bothering me and give up the blame game that goes nowhere. I can try to understand my boss and figure out a way to deal with the situation. Perhaps I need to start looking for another job or perhaps better communication will pave the way for more satisfaction and appreciation for right where I'm at.

It's only when we balance our feelings of inferiority and superiority and open up to compassion and acceptance that we are able to let go of the shame and blame that shrinks our hearts. When we open the door of humility, we welcome in change, learning, and growth and take constructive action. We tear down our defenses, become vulnerable, and embark on a creative journey that will lead to more peace and joy.

Spiritually, humility means relaxing our egos and surrendering to a power greater than ourselves that lives within us. I attended a session on spiritual humility in which we sang a song with the following lyrics: *All that I am, I offer at the altar of love. Sweet Surrender.* Surrender was described as learning how to say "yes" to what is asked. The prayer for surrender was: *Let me understand so I can say yes to what is asked.*

In order to understand, we may need courage to either shut up or speak up. We may need to ask questions and listen, or to voice our genuine thoughts and feelings. Our goal is to open up our minds and our hearts, and in doing so we are inviting in change—and that helps us grow.

We may rejoice in the idea of growth, but shrink from the reality of change. It's so scary to open up to unknown potential and possibility, but it's also so exciting.

Anger at the Situation or God

When we are afraid to open our minds and hearts to change, we may become angry with God or fate. Researchers study at least three types of forgiveness: forgiveness of self, others, and the situation—meaning God or fate.[23] When traumatic events occur we may blame God. "Why did God create such a horrible world? Why didn't God prevent the disease, the war, the hurricane, etc. from happening? Why doesn't God answer my prayers? I've been very specific as to what I desire and I've been a very good person so I deserve better."

Indeed, we are often very specific when we prepare our to-do list for God. God should cure our disease, allow our side to win the war, and make sure the hurricane doesn't hit our house. We know we deserve these things because we've been following the rules we've learned about good behavior. When will God wake up and listen more carefully so our wants and needs are met as we have instructed?

I used to pray for things and give God directions until I gained more humility and realized I really wasn't in any position to know what was best for me or others. There is a delightful Taoist tale that I first heard during a sermon at my Methodist church. It goes as follows.

Story of the Farmer Whose Horse Ran Away

A farmer's horse ran away. On hearing of the misfortune, the farmer's neighbor arrived to commiserate, but all he got from the farmer was, "Who knows what's good or bad?" This proved to be true, for the next day the horse returned bringing with it a drove of wild horses in its train. This time the neighbor arrived with congratulations, only to receive the same response. This too was so, for the next day the farmer's son tried to mount one of the wild horses and broke a leg. More commiserations from the neighbor, with the same response which was again validated, for soldiers soon came around commandeering for the army, and the son was spared because of his injury.

We wish and pray for things we assume are good, but as the story points out, "Who knows what's good or bad?" Now I pray for spiritual help and guidance and I pray that others know I love and support them in their life's journey. I've found it's wiser and safer.

My daughter Jessica was a naturally talented runner, but she hated competition. She loved running during practice and was at the front of the pack. She enjoyed her cross country teammates and they were a large part of her social network. Jessica was a very good runner, so I thought it was my duty as a parent to encourage her to win races and be the best that she could be. I prayed that she would be a successful runner, and my definition of a successful runner at that time was a person who would win races and help their team win championships. Jessica struggled with competitions, while excelling at practice. During meets she suffered stomach pains, and we looked for physical reasons for her problems.

Jessica was chosen to be on the cross country team that went to the state tournament her sophomore year of high school. My husband and I were excited for her and she was anxious to try to please her parents and coach and help the team. What we discovered was that she was too anxious to please. She froze up at the meet and finished near last place. Competition was not her thing. That experience was traumatic for her and she dropped out of cross country and track. She lost her love for running and her social time with teammates.

I was mad at God. Why couldn't God help Jessica do well at races? At that time I didn't entertain the thought that perhaps Jessica needed to follow a different path. I didn't realize that perhaps I was part of the problem, and that good parents didn't always have to encourage their children to be the best but could instead just let them be. I didn't open up to the Spirit. I didn't tell myself, "Who knows what's good or bad?"

I don't tell this story as an admonition regarding the dangers of encouraging your child to do well or develop their talents. Parents can certainly do that with love and kindness. I tell this story because it illustrates the wrong way to pray. My intentions were good, but my mind was closed. I thought I knew what my daughter needed and so instructed God accordingly. But what if I would have prayed differently? What if I would have prayed, "Help me guide and support my daughter. Help me learn from this situation. What should I be opening up to so I understand her stomach pains and her lack of excitement for competition?"

If I had prayed differently—with a more open heart and mind and more humility—perhaps I would have learned a better approach. I may have let Jessica express her fears and concerns more openly. I may have helped her discover a way to enjoy running and her teammates without feeling the need to compete, without worrying about failure or letting down the team or her parents. After a number of years passed, Jessica began to enjoy running again. And her mother learned a better way to pray.

Post-Traumatic Growth

Trauma is no fun. Suffering is no fun. Yet trauma and suffering often lead to growth that is liberating and joyful.

We are each writing our life story, whether or not we put it down on paper. A life story filled only with success and happiness would be a boring read and destined for failure at the box office. I like to read about overcoming obstacles and taking on challenges, and I love a happy ending. When I get to the happy ending, I realize my heroine and hero will encounter future struggles after they cheerfully ride off into the sunset. But I'm counting on them to use their shield of love and compassion to protect them and allow them to keep their happy endings coming.

My favorite thing about humility is that it helps me break through the darkness and find light. I can be my genuine self and relax. I'm not worried about being better or worse than anyone else. I can detach from prideful or shameful thoughts by realizing I am not my thoughts. I can upshift my thinking when my misguided demon (my amygdala, my trickster) sends me messages that are not helpful.

It's Not All about Me

Reminding myself that "It's not all about me," lets me escape my personal prison and find the light. C.S. Lewis is credited with saying, "Humility is not thinking less of yourself, but thinking of yourself less." When I'm focusing on learning and service to others I'm not negatively ruminating about the way things supposedly *should* be or *should have* been. I accept the way things are, work to understand my situation, and figure out how to move ahead compassionately and in a way that honors my moral identity.

Laugh—A Lot!

We certainly wouldn't want to show amusement when heart-felt pain is being expressed. That's a time for shedding tears and listening sympathetically.

Laughter is for our minor forgiveness issues, for instance when I nervously sat on the coffee table instead of the chair for a job interview. Or when my daughter Ashley missed running her only event, the mile, at a track meet I'd been sitting at all day in the rain, because she was so busy socializing with her friends (it took a while to laugh about that one and get over my cold). What a wonderful feeling it is to tell a supportive friend the ridiculous thing you or someone else did, and then laugh with them as they share a ridiculous thing that happened to them as well.

Laughter is the joyful feeling of letting go of expectations and opening up to the unexpected. We laugh because the punch line is not what we expected. Try out the following quotes and see if they make you smile.

I used to think I was indecisive, but now I'm not too sure.

Doing nothing is hard; you never know when you're done.

If two wrongs don't make a right, try three.

My mom had a picture that I now have in my home with the following quote: *Blessed are we who can laugh at ourselves, for we shall never cease to be amused.*

Laughter and humility go together because they are both about the freedom of letting go and enjoying life in all its craziness. We toss out unnecessary fears, open our minds, and let in the light. All is well with our souls.

The next story is about Fadel, a man who found his way to humility by conquering excessive pride and turning his passion for revenge into a passion for understanding. He found the courage to control fearful emotions that were preventing him from opening up his heart and mind to forgiveness and a better way of life.

A Cloud Is Lifted: Fadel's Story

*The single biggest problem in communication
is the illusion that it has taken place.*
—GEORGE BERNARD SHAW

Communication and problem solving are difficult. It's so easy for people to misinterpret what we are saying or doing, and it's just as easy for us to misinterpret what they are saying or doing. We view a situation through the eyes we were given, but our eyes can develop cataracts. Cataracts cloud our vision. If we're fortunate, we can have surgery to lift that cloud, clear our vision, and give us a new lease on life. Learning to forgive can be like having cataract surgery.

Fadel was a 38-year-old educator who grew up Muslim in Iraq. He aided American troops in his country before coming to the United States to live. In his youth Fadel, like many young men, had a lot of pride. Pride can be beneficial when it leads to self-worth and confidently doing good work. But excessive pride leads to what the Greeks call *hubris*, which they warned often comes before a fall. Hubris makes us belligerent because we are intolerant of attacks on the polished armor of perfection we have imagined ourselves shielded by. We strike out at illusory attackers, eager to defend the moral, self-righteous shell we have built around ourselves. Consequently, excessive pride makes it hard to forgive.

Even though Fadel knew Islam encouraged forgiveness, he instead sought revenge when he felt wronged. He told me, "I would try to find any way possible to get back at the person I was angry with and say something hurtful to them. I wanted to make things worse for people I was angry with and didn't think about forgiving."

Fadel explained that in his younger years he just looked at a situation from his own perspective. "If I thought what someone did was awful, I assumed he should come ask me for forgiveness. He was the one who was wrong, so he should come and apologize to me. I didn't think I had any responsibility in the matter."

Fadel's reaction to offensive words or actions was not unusual. Insults threaten our security and create fear. Until we expand and develop the tools in our problem-solving tool box, our instinctual reaction is to lash out at threats or run away from them. In addition, Fadel came from a collectivist, or group-oriented culture, in which honor, respect, and avoiding shame were greatly valued. Fadel's dignity was very important to him and he was sensitive to slights and any statements that he felt lowered his status or in any way demeaned him.

Fadel remembered his first, but definitely not last, experience of forgiving that marked a turning point for him. He had an argument with a very close friend and neighbor that caused him much worry and sadness. I asked him what that argument was about. Fadel responded, "I cannot remember what the argument was about, but we ended up not talking to each other. He said something that violated my personality, my dignity, and I felt insulted."

"What?" I thought, "You can't remember what words caused all that worry and sadness?"

But that's not uncommon. Think of the family feuds and nationalistic antagonisms in which people remember the hate and the hurt, but not necessarily what caused the hurt and why it hurt. We feel offended, but if we don't cognitively process the pain, all we may clearly remember are feelings.

When my daughter Ashley was in kindergarten she came home upset one day. There had been drama at recess between two groups of girls. "I'm so mad at those girls," she said. "My friends and I aren't going to play with them anymore. They were mean to us."

I responded, "Maybe you can talk to them. Listen to why they said what they did and try to work things out."

I thought I gave great advice and was eager to find out how the playground battle would be settled. So when Ashley returned home the next day, I asked if she resolved her problems with the mean girls. She said, "Yes, it was a good day. We played together."

I self-congratulated myself on giving excellent motherly guidance that had led to such quick conflict resolution. Then I asked how the conflict was resolved. "Oh, we couldn't remember why we were mad so we decided to play together."

My short-lived ego balloon quickly deflated, but I was very impressed. What wise children! How often do we hang on to angry, hurt feelings that don't have a solid basis of rational support? It may be wise to let go and forgive if we can't remember exactly why we're hurt or angry, but being that we are human, that may be impossible. If we are feeling angry or hurt, we need to uncover our pain and work on healing.

Forgiveness Is Not Forgetting

If our dignity has been damaged and we are feeling hurt, there's work to be done. Fadel emphasized that true forgiveness is more than not remembering an incident. "Forgiveness is when you remember, but you still forgive that person fully. Forgiveness is very much greater than just forgetting about it."

Although Fadel's cleric, family, and friends had talked to him about forgiveness previously, until the painful incident with his close friend and neighbor, he had not paid much attention to the idea. Pride and anger made him deaf to their words. "We [Muslims] all know we should forgive, because we read our holy book on a daily basis and there are many verses nudging us, encouraging us to forgive people. However, I didn't do that."

So, what changed for Fadel? Fadel felt that one change was simply growing older and wiser. "I started realizing the rewards of forgiving people and began understanding that forgiving is better than not forgiving. I found that forgiving was like the lifting of a burden, the lessening of extra weight."

Developmentally, the time was finally right for Fadel to truly listen to his cleric and others, try out forgiveness, and discover whether there really might be rewards for following sacred scripture. He started becoming more concerned about his spiritual self. The Quran 24:22 states, ". . .and let them forgive and overlook. Would you not like that Allah [God] should forgive you? Allah is Forgiving and Merciful." Fadel wondered, "If I can't forgive, will God forgive me?"

Fadel made the choice to forgive his close friend, even though he didn't really think he was at fault. He decided to forgive because he trusted it was what God wanted him to do, and because he cared about his relationship. But it still took lots of courage for him to actually go talk to his friend.

Courage to Overcome Prideful Emotions

"I thought I should just be a strong person and step over my emotions, my feelings, and go talk to my friend and see what happens. It won't be the end of the world if I do that. I thought—even if he is wrong, I better go talk to him and ask him to forgive me, and I will forgive him. When I did that I stepped over my emotion. There was a strange force trying to prevent it, some psychological force—maybe my pride, my vanity—I don't know.

But I went there and talked to him and I asked him for forgiveness." Overcoming that force allowed Fadel to open his mind and communicate with his friend.

Fadel forgave his close friend and his friend forgave him. It was a reciprocal process that went beyond blame and shame and led to reconciliation. But being forgiving requires continual work as new challenges present themselves.

Fadel again found himself upset and angry because of damaged dignity and offensive words and actions, this time with his best friend. For almost five months the two friends since childhood did not communicate with each other. Fadel experienced the pain of not forgiving and again made the decision to step over his prideful emotions and approach a longtime friend. "I felt that he is my best friend. If I'm not going to forgive him, who am I going to forgive? It makes me a better person when I forgive. I feel much relief when I talk to people I'm angry with. I just cannot walk by and not talk to that person. The best way is to break the ice."

Fadel went to talk to his best friend. I asked what he said to him. "I didn't ask him directly for forgiveness. I started by saying, 'Hey, how are you? I haven't talked to you forever and I miss our conversations. We used to be best friends. So no matter what's happened between us, let's get over it and let's start over.' I also told him, 'God will reward us if we forgive each other.'"

"How did your friend react?" I asked.

"He reacted positively. It was like he was waiting for that moment to come."

Forgiveness Creates Sunny Days

"It's like a secret touch when you forgive people," said Fadel. "When I'm not forgiving, I feel I'm not really myself—not in my full intelligent mind. There's something blocking me from seeing the other person directly, seeing him clearly. But after forgiving, a cloud goes away and I can communicate better with that person. I understand him or her better."

"How do you make the cloud go away?" I probed.

"I've learned to respect opinions that differ from my own and take offensive comments less seriously. People don't always have to agree with me. And I realize that at certain times people say things they don't really mean. So it's better not to judge people when they are super mad. Wait until they calm down to discuss issues."

Fadel worked to control his emotions and not take things too earnestly. "I have to be ruled by reason, not by passion. I cannot be mad at people every time they say something I don't like. I have to understand where she or he came from and process an incident before I react. Reading books, talking about religion and culture, and interacting with a variety of people has helped me better understand people."

Forgiveness Means Taking Responsibility

Fadel became more compassionate and understanding of others, which helped him forgive. I asked him if he has also become more forgiving of himself. He explained that he is wary of self-forgiveness. "I don't forgive myself easily. I have high standards for myself and am tougher on myself than I am on others. I take full responsibility for my mistakes and I think that helps me accomplish more."

Taking responsibility for his mistakes was important to Fadel and facilitated his achievement and growth. It also contributed to his ability to forgive others. "It makes me more humble. Hey, I'm full of mistakes. I'm not a better person than others."

"Is forgiveness hard?" I inquired.

"It's really hard. Most of us are ruled by our emotions and feelings. And forgiving, it's actually stepping through those feelings and emotions that are like a concrete door blocking your ability to forgive. And I think it happens on a daily basis. So if we don't forgive, things will fall apart and we could lose everything. Having the courage and spending the time needed to forgive may prevent you from destroying your life or the life of another person. Open the channels of communication. See if there are any options, any conditions that may help you resolve your problems."

Fadel made the decision to forgive because he realized the rewards of forgiveness were greater than the costs. He decided to quit worrying about who was at fault, quit letting excessive pride hold him hostage, quit hiding behind a cloud of emotions that had prevented him from moving forward. Deciding to forgive means we have the courage to embark on an effortful process with faith that it is morally the right thing to do, and that it will eventually lead us to better health, relationships, and growth.

WORK TO UNDERSTAND WITH COMPASSION

Compassion does not just happen.
Pity does, but compassion is not pity. It's not a feeling.
Compassion is a viewpoint, a way of life, a perspective,
a habit that becomes a discipline—and more than
anything else, compassion is a choice we make that
love is more important than comfort or convenience.
—GLENNON DOYLE MELTON

Piaget, a famous developmental psychologist, theorized that one of childhood's developmental milestones is to overcome egocentrism, meaning the inability to understand another person's viewpoint or behavior. It's hard for young children to understand a perspective other than their own because, after all, they are still working to figure out what their own perspective is. As adults, we have the ability to overcome egocentrism, but we don't always choose to do so.

As Melton said, compassion is not just about feeling sorry for someone and it's definitely not about justifying bad behavior. Compassion means actively working to understand and alleviate pain. Compassion guides us to forgiveness.

The Dalai Lama said, "A truly compassionate attitude toward others does not change even if they behave negatively or hurt you." Therein lies the challenge. When people hurt us, it's hard to be interested in their perspective. We want to use our energy to protect ourselves instead of working on kindly understanding the reasons for their behavior.

Why would we want to have compassion for the people who are hurting us? Albert Einstein said, "A human being is a part of the whole called by us universe, a part limited in time and space. He experiences himself, his thoughts and feelings as something separated from the rest, a kind of optical delusion of his consciousness. This delusion is a kind of prison for us, restricting us to our personal desires and to affection for a few persons nearest to us. Our task must be to free ourselves from this prison by widening our circle of compassion to embrace all living creatures and the whole of nature in its beauty."

The Jewish Jerusalem Talmud, Nedarim 9.4, speaks to the unity and oneness of all people and describes vengeance as a person "who, having cut one hand while handling a knife, avenges himself by stabbing the other hand" (as cited in Freke, 1998, p. 79). Believing in the oneness of all people with God makes vengeance ludicrous and compassion wise.

The Buddha said, "In separateness lies the world's great misery, in compassion lies the world's true strength." It's natural to want to separate ourselves from those we deem harmful or morally inferior. And we may need to physically separate from dangerous people. But the Buddha was not talking about letting ourselves be harmed, he was talking about letting ourselves be open to new understandings that will bring us strength. We are all connected to each other whether we like it or not, and it's compassion that makes this at worst tolerable and at best joyful.

Being open to new understandings can be aided when we remember we too have failings. Mahatma Gandhi, a Hindu, stated his tolerance of those who oppressed him stemmed from awareness of his own failings. The Hindu scripture, Ramayana, Yuddha Kanda 115 states, "A noble soul will ever exercise compassion even toward those who enjoy injuring others or those of cruel deeds when they are actually committing them—for who is without fault?" (as cited in Freke, 1998, p. 78).

We have every good reason in the world to condemn a hurtful behavior or painful event. Evil happens. We don't forgive the evil action; we work to forgive people like ourselves who are capable of both good and evil. Compassion means recognizing that poor behavior and suffering are part of the human condition, and understanding that kindness and curiosity have the power to lessen our pain and brighten our lives. That's why Maya Angelou advised, "Forgive everybody. It's one of the greatest gifts you can give yourself, to forgive."

Compassion is necessary for forgiveness because it means understanding others or ourselves with loving kindness, and realizing hatred harms our soul and revenge creates more problems than it solves. We can't forgive and let go of our damaging feelings unless we understand them and act on them in a way that will alleviate suffering.

When I am not feeling compassionate, and bitterness or fear is creeping into my head and heart, I like to remember quotes from the forgiveness heroes I interviewed. My favorite from Rose, whom you will meet next, is, "No one is going to make me hate." That statement reminds me I have a choice. I can choose light or I can choose darkness; love and compassion or hatred and revenge. I can choose forgiveness.

No One Can Make You Hate: Rose's Story

If you want others to be happy, practice compassion.
If you want to be happy, practice compassion.
—DALAI LAMA

Rose was a 66-year-old Lakota woman who was an educator and Sacred Pipe Carrier. Sacred Pipe carriers are individuals who have been walking their journey on earth in an admirable way for many years and have accepted the responsibility that goes with the honor. She was walking the Red Road, which is a Native American metaphor for living a spiritual way of life. Walking the Red Road means living your life with purpose and being guided by seven sacred virtues: prayer, honesty, humility, compassion, respect, generosity, and wisdom.

Rose's mother, Irene, and pregnant sister, Judy, both of whom she was close to, were brutally murdered in their apartment about thirty years before our interview. Both were stabbed with a blunt instrument, which was believed to be a screwdriver, sixty to seventy times. They were victims of someone's rage and anger.

Rose's sister was three months pregnant and unmarried when the event happened. Judy had called Rose a few weeks before the murder to tell her she was with child. She was happy about the pregnancy, but concerned because she did not want to marry the child's father. He was an alcoholic and she knew his lifestyle would create a poor environment for their child. Rose had volunteered to help raise the child and had assured Judy that extended family would provide her with assistance.

Rose had much respect for her mother, whom she described as very intelligent and talented. Irene was well-educated and a teacher. During her early years, Irene had been strong and a great role model, but the last several years of her life had been difficult. Rose remembered the heart-to-heart conversation she had with her mother a week before the murder and her mother's last words to her.

"Always remember the values that you were taught when you were young, Rose. Our traditional Lakota values. Always be truthful to people. Be compassionate. Be respectful."

"Yes, Mom. I won't forget those. They are ingrained in how we believe. I won't forget them."

"All right. I love you very much. Always remember that."

"I love you too. I really love you."

Rose was grateful for that conversation and still thinks about it. "When I look back on that now, I wonder if Mom felt that it may have been the last time she would be able to visit with me."

A week after the conversation Rose, her husband Tom, and their two sons were at home when they noticed that a friend, Bill, kept driving by their house. Rose told Tom, "I think Bill must want to talk to you about something. He keeps driving by the house, but for some reason he hasn't stopped."

The incident took place before cell phones were plentiful, plus, Rose noted, "We were kind of pitiful. We were poor. We had one working vehicle and we were living hand to mouth. We were just having a hard time. So we didn't have a phone at home, a landline. And I had thought, 'That's okay, I've got a phone at work I can use when I need to make a call.'"

Bill stopped eventually, but still didn't come in. He just sat outside in the driveway. Rose told Tom, "You better go out there. He's not coming in." Tom went outside, talked to Bill, and then came back in. Rose could tell by his sad, serious face that it was not good news.

"You have to sit down, Rose."

"Something happened, right, something bad?"

"Yes, it's bad. It's very bad. But—but we'll get through it." Rose and Tom's life had not been easy and they had been through tough times together, drawing on each other's strengths. Tom felt crushed by the horror of the news he was bearing, but he was also determined that their family would persevere.

"I'll sit down," responded Rose.

Rose's husband gave her the terrible news and said, "We'll find out what happened, but for now, we'll just sit here."

"No," replied Rose. "I need to go upstairs to the prayer room."

"Okay," said Tom, understanding Rose's need for spiritual comfort and stillness. "Go to the prayer room. I'll watch the boys. You go up and pray."

Rose stayed in the prayer room for at least an hour while Tom watched their two sons, the youngest of whom was only a few months old. "The only reason I left the prayer room," Rose reflected, "is because I wanted to hold my sons."

Rose felt a key to her healing was following her instincts and immediately seeking spiritual solace and guidance. "I think if I had not gone into that prayer room and prayed—prayed really hard about it—I think my heart would have hardened. My gut was telling me to go pray. I'm glad I followed my intuition because it saved me, and it has taught me how to deal with other difficult things in my life."

Choose Forgiveness Before Your Heart Can Harden

Rose intuitively knew it was important that she choose compassion and forgiveness as soon as possible—before her heart could harden. "I prayed for my loved ones and I prayed for their killers. I had my Pipe there in my hand and I clutched it and I prayed with it. I brought the Pipe down and I smoked it with my husband. I kept praying that my mom and sister didn't suffer and that they died quickly. I hated the thought of them suffering."

Rose decided right away to make the decision to forgive. Making the decision to forgive didn't mean she immediately was able to let go of her pain and feel fine. Rose knew she had hard emotional and spiritual work ahead of her. But she made the decision to start healing because forgiveness, courage, and compassion were vital to her belief system and moral identity. Her sacred beliefs guided her and allowed her to process the horrendous event that had occurred in an ethical manner. Her support system gave her the courage to work through her pain and eventually let go so she could emotionally forgive—so, as she described, her heart would not harden.

When we can't forgive, our heart can metaphorically shrink, causing our health to deteriorate and our relationships to become harsh. We can't be a light to others when we are locked in the dark cage of unforgiveness.

As I was writing about Rose, I realized why it can be so important to make the decision to forgive as soon as possible. Forgiveness is valuable at any time in our lives, but habits and patterns of thinking can be difficult to change. Forgiveness will be easier if we prevent damaging thoughts and behaviors from taking control of us. We can choose to take the difficult, but productive path of forgiveness right away and save ourselves from tripping on the seductive, but unhealthy, revenge or repression detour.

Rose's personal understanding of spirits and the afterlife helped her cope with the tragedy. One of her grandfathers, who was a medicine man—a holy man—taught her, "A body is just a physical shell. It is not your soul. It's not your spirit."

"I know there are spirits," said Rose, "and I felt that my mother, sister, and the baby went to a good place. I continue to pray for them and remember them in ceremonies. Their spirits are with us."

Was justice ever done? Was there closure regarding the murders? Rose said, "My sister's ex-boyfriend, the father of the child, was on trial for the murders, but never convicted. There were two hung juries."

Rose thought it probable that the estranged boyfriend was responsible for the murders. "My sister told me she had separated from the baby's father and she had informed him she was not going to raise a child with him because he was an alcoholic and was using drugs. She did not want to live that kind of lifestyle."

Rose had a dream in which three murky looking men were in the apartment and took part in the murders. One of the men appeared to be her sister's estranged boyfriend. Rose said, "It was apparent in my dream that the men were not in their right minds at the time of the deaths. I believe they were on drugs, they were high. I can truly say I feel sorry for whoever did it. I have compassion for them. I wish justice had been done and that they had been held accountable, but I did not have control over that and I didn't want that injustice to have control over me."

How do you have compassion for someone who brutally murders your mother and pregnant sister? It goes against our instincts to feel compassion for those who cause great pain to us or our loved ones. Our tendency is to see those people as objects that cause hurt, not as human beings who are hurting. We want to punish them or damage them in some way, believing that will make us safer and take away our pain. We may seethe with resentment and lash out at others, not realizing the cycle of hatred we are creating.

Pray for Those Who Hurt You

Rose wisely chose the productive path of compassion and forgiveness over vengeance and retribution. She prayed for the murderer or murderers. "People asked me if I prayed that something bad would happen to whoever murdered my mother and sister. I said, 'No. I never pray *against* anyone. It serves no purpose to be vengeful and seek to hurt those who hurt us. It's not for me to be the judge. Maybe the person was not in his right mind. Maybe he doesn't even remember doing it. Maybe he is mentally ill. I can't judge the behavior of others.'"

"What did you pray?" I asked.

"I prayed for the souls of the murderer or murderers. I prayed that whoever did it will find peace—will find their right path in life so they can make their own amends to their Creator. I've had people say, 'I can't believe that you forgave.' But I say, 'It's based on my belief system and the Pipe and how we are taught. We must act the way we believe. I can't say that I'm a Pipe Carrier if I don't act accordingly. I don't want to be a hypocrite.'"

Rose's belief system provided her with a forgiveness foundation. "We know that we are only human, and because we are human, we will make mistakes," said Rose. "But we should learn from our mistakes. We should not continue to repeat them."

I asked Rose to explain how the Pipe is important to her. "The Pipe is very symbolic. It's a reminder of Lakota traditional beliefs, and is similar in importance to the Christian symbol of the cross. The Pipe as a symbol reminds me that it is not my role as a human being to judge others. They have to come to terms with who the Creator is in their own minds. They have to choose how to deal with their own situations. We cannot walk in anyone else's shoes. We can only walk in our own. It's hard enough walking in my own."

Belief Based on Faith, Not Certainty

Processing forgiveness issues that involve death means confronting an area of belief based on faith, not certainty. No one alive knows with certainty what happens when we die. None of the people I interviewed claimed to know exactly what happens when it's time to leave our earthly bodies, but most felt there was an afterlife of some kind. They felt our job now is to learn and grow and live the best life we can.

Forgiveness can be difficult to describe. Words and logic only go so far. Rose said, "Sometimes it's difficult to explain to people why and how I forgive. My beliefs are in my heart. They're a part of me. I don't analyze everything. Some things are just part of the way it is."

There were songs at the funeral of Rose's mother and sister as well as prayers for their souls. One of Rose's sisters, who was at the funeral and who was Catholic, had a comforting experience during that time of song and prayer. Rose's sister told her, "You may not believe me, but I'm going to tell you what I saw while you were singing and praying. A white buffalo [sacred to the

NO ONE CAN MAKE YOU HATE: | 151

Lakota] emerged between the two caskets. It went up towards the ceiling and became like a cloud. It then disappeared and I saw what appeared to be spirits also rise right after that and fade through the ceiling."

To Rose's sister, the vision was a message that her loved ones had gone to heaven and were okay. Because she understood they were all right, she could move ahead with forgiveness. Forgiveness gave both Rose and her sister peace, but they will never forget. Rose stated, "Both of us say we can't forget, but we understand."

Forgiveness Takes Away an Offender's Power to Hurt Us

Forgiveness is not forgetting. Forgiveness takes away a memory's power to hurt us. Forgiveness transforms a memory so we can learn, grow, and move forward.

Rose was a bit surprised that the vision appeared to her sister, who was Catholic, but the vision was consistent with Lakota traditional beliefs. Rose's grandfather had advised her to always look up at funerals, not down. He said, "When someone dies, people often look down at the grave or pray with their heads down. You should look up instead because you may see something very miraculous." Rose remembered her grandpa's advice and said, "When I go to funerals and wakes, especially when people are buried, I look up. I look up in the sky and see wonderful things. Oftentimes, I'll see an eagle flying around carrying prayers or some other positive symbol."

Forgiveness of a major offense will always be hard, but we can develop a forgiveness disposition that allows us to forgive more freely. Forgiving her family's murderer(s) was extremely hard, but it transformed Rose. "I've gotten angry at certain situations and things, but since this incident, I've always worked to resolve situations in a positive way. I realize that some people have not reached a point of self-worth or self-actualization. Everybody is essentially different and I can't judge people because I don't understand their particular situation and what level they are at in their lives."

Rose was an example of humility and forgiveness from a young age. She related to me an experience with her grandmother that brought tears to my eyes as well as deep admiration.

"There was an earlier incident that I remember with my grandmother when I was probably about nine or ten years old. I was bright enough to know what was going on, but it took me a minute to process it. We had gone to eat in a restaurant, just my grandma and I. Both of us are easily identified as American Indians. In the restaurant the waitress kept walking past us—she wouldn't give us the menu or anything. She just kept walking. Finally I stopped her and said, 'Ma'am, are you going to give us a menu?' The waitress looked right through me and said, 'Well, I don't think so.'"

"I'll never forget how that experience affected my grandmother. Tears were coming down her face. I never really analyzed it with her because I was so young, but I think she felt bad because that was one of my first experiences with racism. My grandma was in her sixties so of course she'd dealt with it. I think my grandma was sad for me and I was sad for my grandma."

Rose remembered her thoughts about the waitress. "You are really ignorant because you don't want to serve us. We have money to spend here. And you are mean. My grandma is a beautiful lady. I love her dearly and you made her cry."

Rose's grandma said, "Maybe we should leave."

Rose responded loudly so all the people sitting by them could hear. "We're going to leave. Let's go. If they're not going to serve us because we're American Indian, then we don't have to spend our money here."

Rose recollected, "My grandma looked a little bit embarrassed that I did that, but afterward she said that she was proud of me. I've always been a little bit outspoken."

Rose reflected that forgiveness was easy in that situation because she perceived the waitress as ignorant and because she had been able to stand up for herself and her grandmother. "The waitress did not have the sense to know that we are human beings," Rose explained, "and we just came to eat like everyone else."

Rose was assertive, but not aggressive or mean. She learned how to deal with people who judged her negatively based simply on her Native American heritage. How was she able to deal with racist actions? "You either get consumed by hatred or handle it in a positive way," Rose said. "I'll be darned if anybody is going to make me hate myself or hate anybody else. I knew from an early age that that's not how I was going to live my life. Nobody was going to control me."

Lack of Knowledge Prevents Compassion

Rose realized that sometimes people don't have an understanding of another group of people. "Lack of knowledge prevents compassion. People are just not educated about us [American Indians]." Rose didn't like being judged by people who didn't understand her, and she chose not to mimic that behavior.

Rose was grateful for her parents, who raised her and her siblings to be proud of their American Indian heritage. "My parents told us we have the ability to do whatever we want," explained Rose. "They were very important role models, as were my grandparents and extended family. I have some really strong women in my extended family who have been key role models in my life. I watched how they conducted themselves, how they spoke, and how they handled different situations. They taught me a lot."

Rose appreciated and respected her relatives. She is now motivated to be a good role model herself. "I want to be a good example for my children and the Lakota people. I want them to be proud of me. I'm careful not to tarnish the image of our *tiospaye* [extended family]."

"What are some important aspects of your sacred belief system that help you forgive?" I probed.

"I was taught that all life is sacred and that the things you do in your life affect the people around you. We are all connected so it's important we are careful with what we say and do. We can connect with each other and the Creator through prayer and we can pray in different ways. We can pray through crying, through oratory, through songs with people and communion with others who are also crying. What we call the Silent Prayer is just letting out that which is within your heart and soul. Prayer helps clear our minds and can create positive energy. That's why it's important not to inadvertently create negative energy by praying for something that's judgmental or harmful to others."

Quieting Our Minds

Prayer is a universal spiritual practice and it reflects the significance of quieting the mind. Quieting the mind is an important concept in psychology as well. We don't have the capacity to think clearly when we're fearful, anxious, or distracted.

Calming our minds means taking a break from busyness and activity for reflection or meditation. This can be difficult in our society, where it seems everyone strives to be very busy because being busy is equated with productivity and happiness. But is that always the case?

"Some people are afraid to be still," Rose noted. "In my adult life I've found that people often like chaos and lots of noisy distractions. They always have to have their iPods or some type of gadget going. They're looking at Facebook, or Twitter, or something. They can't just sit and chill. Just be quiet or go on a hike or go to a quiet place in their home. I think everybody needs to do that. But that's my bias, I guess. I believe everybody has to connect with themselves at one point or another."

Busyness can help us avoid facing tough issues, as can alcohol, pills, and other diversions. But our pain won't go away unless we are brave enough to wrestle with it. "If you harbor hatred or negative feelings towards someone or some event, whatever it is, then it only eats at your heart," said Rose.

Dealing with a painful situation and connecting with ourselves can be daunting. That's why forgiveness takes courage and compassion. We have to take a look into our souls and make peace with the parts of us that are scary. The parts that are afraid, angry, resentful, ashamed, humiliated, or embarrassed. And we need to treat those scary parts of ourselves with kindness and compassion if we want to lighten our burdens and brighten our outlooks.

Prayer helped Rose be at peace with herself and sustained her daily. "Every day I thank the Creator for the blessings in my life and the gifts I have been given. I ask the Creator's help in using my gifts in a good way so I can help my people live."

"Who do you include as your people?"

"When we say 'the people,' we mean all people, not just people who are Lakota," explained Rose. "That's how I was taught to pray, especially in ceremony but also every day. *Mitakuye Oyasin* are Lakota words that reflect the world view that we are all related and interconnected."

If We Don't Know Ourselves Well, We Can Be Easily Tricked

Rose displayed compassion for all people as she realized that we human beings can be easily tricked, especially if we don't know ourselves well. We may tell ourselves lies, and we may tell others lies if we cannot understand and accept who we are.

"We Lakota have stories about Iktomi. In Lakota mythology, Iktomi is a spider-trickster spirit. We all have Iktomis that like to cause trouble and trick us into doing things we shouldn't. If we continue to lie to ourselves and others about our behavior, things only get worse and worse and worse. On the other hand, if we tell the truth and seek the truth and seek the light, things work out a lot better. Always look to the light in life and in people. Don't become one of the people that walk around with little clouds over their heads, living a negative life. I feel bad for them. I feel sad for them. They have not been able to find peace in life."

Rose was aware of the dangers of negative, hateful thinking. She was also aware that if you take off the negative, you need to replace it with something positive. In Lakota tradition, burning or smudging with sage symbolizes healing and taking the negative off, while sweetgrass represents blessings and putting on something positive. We can take off our bitterness and shame and replace it with acts of kindness and thankful thoughts.

Rose's sacred beliefs, prayers, and solid family and spiritual attachments gave her the courage, compassion, and creativity she needed to forgive. She viewed life through a wide angle lens and said, "We're not here on earth very long so live each day the best that you can and nurture love, not hate; gratitude, not negativity; forgiveness, not revenge."

The next person you will meet, Valerie, was a strong woman of the Baha'i faith who, like Rose, exemplified the beauty of compassion. When I am discouraged, saddened, or angry at someone's behavior—my own included—I remind myself of my favorite quote from Valerie: "We are all on our own paths."

WE ARE ALL ON OUR OWN PATHS: VALERIE'S STORY

Understanding
Understanding has its own pace.
It can be nurtured and cultivated,
But it cannot be hurried or forced.
Understanding develops according to its own seasons,
And once it blooms the result is beautiful.

Valerie was a compassionate 66-year-old woman who was guided by her Baha'i faith and supported by her intimate Baha'i community. The Baha'i Faith was established in 1863 by the prophet Bahá'u'lláh, whom Baha'i view as the latest of God's messengers, all coming from the same Source. Valerie's experiences in life and her openness to learning helped her grow in patience and acceptance of others. She realized we are all following unique paths and need more support than judgment along the way.

We sat down to talk in Valerie's kitchen and I asked her to share what she considered was her most significant forgiveness experience. Her response surprised me. She chose forgiving a boss who had terminated her employment from a job she didn't like. You might think she must have had an easy life if a bad boss was her worst offender. But Valerie had been raped and suffered abuse much worse than that inflicted by the owner of the store where she had previously worked.

Reflecting back, Valerie said, "I've had lots of experiences with people who've done terrible things to me, but I've maintained a strong belief in the importance of forgiveness because none of us are perfect. This event pops out because it seems so incredibly strange to me that I would have held a grudge against this one person for so long over something that in the big scheme of things was so trivial."

The pain and hurt we feel surrounding an event is based on a number of factors and is relative. What seems unforgiveable to one person may be perceived as minor to another. Our ability to empathize with and understand our offender, our subjective assessment of the harm caused, and our perceived ability to cope with an offense affect the intensity of pain we are feeling. Closeness of the relationship may be influential because we are often more highly motivated to maintain attachments with family and friends. Processing transgressions involving close relationships may be easier because we have a better opportunity to understand our offender and the situation. Valerie explained how those factors impacted her experience.

"My husband and I both lost our jobs in the same week. It was the biggest fluke ever. So we were both on unemployment, looking for work. The unemployment office sent me to a local business to apply for a retail job a couple months before Christmas. I had been selling my personal items because we were desperate for money, so I really didn't have nice clothes. I also had just found out I was pregnant. Not a good time for that!"

"I went on the interview in my jeans and tennis shoes and wasn't excited about the job. They hired me anyway and I had to take the job because we needed the money. I wasn't a real good fit for the position and thought some of the store policies were racist. For example, their policy was that if a white person was writing a check, all that was needed was a driver's license with picture ID. That was simple. If you were a person of color though, especially Native American, they wanted you to have the driver's license plus two credit cards, one with a picture on it. This was back in 1980, but people still don't have pictures on their credit cards."

"How did you handle that?"

"I just refused to comply because I would look at those people and think, 'I'm white but they're doing much better financially than me.' So I would just ask for their license and take down their license number, and if they didn't have a phone number on the check I'd put that on there. I treated everyone the same. I never had a check come back on me."

Valerie worked full-time until after Christmas when things slowed down. The owner decided not as many employees were needed after the holidays so Valerie was let go. She again filed for unemployment but, much to her surprise, the owner of the store disputed it.

"I was not prepared at all for the hearing. The employer presented a list of dates that I had been sick. I knew I had been sick a lot during my pregnancy, but I didn't think I'd really missed many days of work. I didn't have a calendar with me and was unable to dispute the dates given at the hearing. When I had a chance to check the days they listed, I found that most of them were Mondays, which was my day off. And two of the days were after they terminated my employment. I lost my unemployment and I was really upset because we needed the money so badly. They fired another girl just because she wasn't home on her day off and they needed somebody to fill in. It's like they really didn't care about us."

Valerie was naturally upset because her employer had not been truthful at the hearing and the consequence of that put her and her husband in a very tough financial situation. There were other reasons she felt so angry at the store owner.

"The owner of the store made all the decisions, but he had his manager, who was a tiny lady, do all the dirty work. It really bothered me that he wouldn't deal with problems himself. He was a coach for youth sports teams and everybody in the neighborhood had such high regard for him, but I'd look at him and my blood would boil. Anytime I'd even hear his name I'd feel angry and bitter. I got into a vicious cycle of almost hatred. It impacted me more than other terrible things I've been through."

Forgiveness is about mercy, but it's also about justice. Valerie never saw justice. The owner of the store cheated her out of unemployment compensation and had no consequences for his bad behavior. To make it worse, people around her thought he was a nice guy. She never confronted the man about his behavior, or developed an understanding of who he was as a person. He was simply an object that had caused her pain and she had felt helpless and unable to defend herself against his actions.

Valerie knew our interview was coming up and she had been reflecting on her experience. "I've been thinking about it the past few days and I think that I didn't confront my unforgiveness because it seemed I shouldn't be bothered by the event. Consequently I didn't give it the proper consideration that it deserved. I mean, people have actually done criminal things against me and I was able to forgive them because I prayed about it. Prayer is a really important part of forgiveness for me. This incident just went by me without much conscious thought because it seemed like it shouldn't be affecting me. It wasn't a really horrible incident, like other things that had happened to me. However, it impacted me more."

Escape from a Dark Place

Emotionally forgiving a major transgression takes effort. Valerie was angry at her boss, but didn't put in the time and energy needed to face the issue and determine how to deal with her destructive emotions. Her wounds festered for 16 years, until forgiving another painful incident freed her from the bitterness she'd stored inside for her former boss.

"We moved away from the city where the owner of the store lived, so I didn't have to hear his name, see him, or have much contact with him. I kind of forgot about him until my daughter and her husband and their two kids came to stay with us for a while. One day all our children were gathered in our home and the son-in-law who was staying with us started acting so horribly. He insulted me in front of my five adult children and used such vulgar language. He accused me of terrible things and I felt just awful. He was shaming me in front of my children. I thought, 'Oh, my gosh! What am I going to do about this?' He was damaging our family relations. This wasn't trivial.'"

"So after a couple of days I thought, 'Okay, I have this one prayer that in times of real trial, I say nine times. It's a long prayer. I'm going to try that.' So I prayed and within maybe a few hours, I felt like this burden was lifted from me. I didn't feel any animosity towards my son-in-law. And the prayer was powerful because the next time I came in contact with my former boss I didn't feel angry towards him either. I thought, 'Wow! This is great.'"

"Tell me about your prayer."

"It's a very, very special prayer for me and I say it every day now, because times are tough. The prayer reminds me there is only one God and we are all members of the same human family. God is eternal and will always be there to guide us. We can turn away from God or we can turn towards God—it's our choice. Part of it says, 'Even if heaven and earth should rise against you, be thou the flame of fire to my enemies so that you would be like a light to them. Be a river of life eternal to my loved ones. Be a person who is kind and helpful. Do not be of those who doubt, have faith.'"

"Can you describe how your thoughts changed about your son-in-law and your former boss after you prayed and had a change of heart?"

"I really can't. All I know is that prayer is very powerful. It changed my heart, how I felt inside. It felt wonderful. I was very grateful because it helped so much."

Some things are hard to explain with words, and I am reminded of the fact that words are symbols. Meaning is in people, not words. Valerie's prayer reminded her we are all connected to each other and that we choose the type of person we want to be. Prayer was a plea for spiritual help that guided her escape from the dark place she had been in and illuminated a new path. She felt the change very deeply, in a way that was hard for her to describe.

Forgiveness involves thoughts, emotions, and behaviors, so I asked Valerie, "How did forgiveness change your behaviors and actions?"

"I was able to speak to my son-in-law after that without hostility, and later I wrote him a letter letting him know I'd forgiven him. I didn't know the owner of the store personally so have never talked with him about the situation, but I've heard people talk about him and I don't respond bitterly. The anger is gone."

Taking Action and Becoming Empowered through Prayer

"What does your forgiveness experience mean to you now?" I asked.

"I go right to prayer. If something is hurting me, even if it seems trivial, I don't waste time anymore. Prayer helps me get rid of the anger and leads me to ways of helping people. It leads me to pleasant, positive experiences."

"How do you conceptualize prayer?" I asked.

"I believe we go on beyond this life, and those who have gone before us help us here in some way. Maybe they pass our prayers on up to a higher level. When my mother was close to death she was suffering a lot and her breathing was so labored. I prayed to God to 'Please, just let her go.' And I felt something like a hand on my shoulder and a voice inside me—not audible—saying, 'It's not time yet.' I've had experiences like this throughout my life."

Valerie gave another example of feeling spiritually connected and protected during a difficult event. "I was raped once and as it was going on something inside me was telling me, 'Nobody can touch you, he can't touch you.'"

I probed, "You mean like a voice inside you that said he can't touch the inner you—the real you?"

"Yes. And so I was never stigmatized by the experience. I just figured out how to get out of that situation as quickly as possible, and I learned to be more cautious with men in the future."

In the case of the rape, Valerie felt able to cope with the offense plus she felt protected at a spiritual level. She learned from her experience and became better prepared to handle sexually dangerous situations in the future. She had experienced growth and felt safe, which enabled her to forgive.

Even if we are not religious, we can open our minds and reflect on why and how something is happening to us that we do not like. We can open our hearts and admit we need help, we need compassion, and let positive energy flow within us.

Sometimes we may need to "fake it until we make it," meaning take healing action and trust that heart and mind will follow. Valerie related a story to me about a family she met in Brazil that was having family problems. They went to a shaman who told them to wash their entire house with salt to get rid of all the bad feelings. "It didn't sound logical to me, but I thought, 'Well, if they believed it would work, at least they're taking action in a positive direction.'"

"Did it work?"

"Yes, and I think it's because they were doing something. They were active. And that's what prayer is, prayer is active. It empowers us."

"How would you describe the role of spirituality and religion in your forgiveness experience?"

"It's paramount. As a Baha'i, I believe that religion should be a way of life. Our material bodies are temporary, but our spiritual being is eternal. We need to develop our spiritual attributes because that's what we are going to need for the next world. Forgiveness is one of those attributes."

"Is your religious community supportive?"

"Oh, yes. We're a close community because there are so few of us. I have a friend who is very supportive and that I have known almost as long as my husband. We agree that it's really nice to have a group of people who accept you, warts and all."

Compassion May Mean Persistence, Discernment, and Patience
Valerie related to me a story from her religion that inspired her and taught her about forgiveness. It involved Abdul Baha, the son of Baha'u'llah, founder of the Baha'i faith.

"Abdul Baha tried to befriend a man who was poor, often in need of food and clothes, and he did many kind acts for the man. Nevertheless, the man hated him because they were of different religions and he felt Abdul Baha was a heretic. The man became very sick and Abdul Baha brought in doctors and medicine to heal him. The man recovered but persisted in his contempt for Abdul Baha. Finally, after twenty-four years, the man had a change of heart. He apologized to Abdul Baha and begged his forgiveness for the wrong he had done to him. They became friends. I especially like that story because it reminds me forgiveness and a change of heart can take a long time."

Prayer and her spiritual connections helped Valerie forgive, but she revealed there was still hard work involved in forgiving tough issues. "You have to analyze a situation and decide what's most important to you. It's challenging in family relationships to determine when to speak up and how to discuss painful words and actions. With my son-in-law I had to be careful because I didn't want to destroy my daughter's marriage or hurt their two kids. I wanted to maintain harmony. Sometimes I choose to prioritize what I think is best for my family over my personal feelings."

Valerie felt the hardest thing about forgiveness was processing a transgression and figuring out how to move forward morally and with compassion. It's not always easy to obtain all the information we need to understand a situation. Plus communication can be tricky.

"One of my kids has just gone through some marital problems and they seem bizarre to me," said Valerie. "So it's taking me a while to process what's going on. If you're not really clear about a situation you can kind of forgive, but it will be temporary until you can really process the information and understand better. Forgiveness involves inner reaction so if you haven't truly figured things out and processed in-depth, you won't be able to emotionally forgive. You may want to forgive, but you're not sure exactly how to approach a person or situation."

Valerie differentiated decisional forgiveness from in-depth forgiveness and being able to truly let go of something. Until we understand a situation and learn how to move forward morally and productively, we will have to grapple with the issues and put forth time and energy.

Valerie noted that when family relationships are difficult, it's important to keep trying to communicate. She recommended using any opportunity to interact with persons you want to better understand so you can be forgiving. "I've had family members do things that are really hard for me to wrap my head around.

I try to face those persons, but not be confrontational. I try to be loving. I want them to know I loved them yesterday, still love them today, and will love them tomorrow. I try to keep the positive part of our relationship intact."

Forgiveness Is Developmental

Forgiveness can be viewed as a developmental concept.[24] Our ability to forgive and the meaning we attach to forgiveness changes with time.[25] I asked Valerie, "Was there a turning point in your life that helped you become more forgiving?"

"The birth of my first child was very significant. It turned me into a grown-up and changed my relationship with my mother, whom I'd been terrible to. Before the birth I was very critical and unforgiving of my mother. My dad traveled a lot and when he was home he spoiled me rotten, and so my mom had tried to compensate for that by being a disciplinarian. I got to a point where I thought I hated her and was very mean to her. My dad died when I was in my teens and that was hard on my mom and me."

"When did your relationship with your mom change?"

"When she stood by me through my first pregnancy, even though I wasn't married. She was with me all through my labor. I was in terrible pain and the drugs they gave me for the pain just made me feel crazy. My mother prayed for me the whole time. I finally gave birth and fell asleep. When I woke up I felt differently toward my mom and never had a problem with our relationship from that day on. I went from resenting my mom to loving her absolutely."

Valerie gained more compassion and gratitude for her mother as she became older. Researchers have linked the ability to empathize with age because we can better understand what others are thinking and feeling when we have been through similar experiences. By becoming a parent herself, Valerie gained empathy for her mom. She remembered how mean she was as a teenager when troubles arose with her own children. That helped her be a forgiving mother.

"I learned from that experience and decided I was not going to take anything my children said to me personally. Even when they said, 'I hate you, Mom.' Because all kids will say that at least once in their life. I didn't mean half of what I said when I was a stupid teenager. This trick worked fine for me and I've told my children about it. But it doesn't seem to work for them. They take what their kids say to them quite personally and get so upset about it."

A trick to forgiving is remembering that the people who lash out at us are probably fearful or hurting inside, and may not have much control over their own emotions. Valerie was able to do that. It is not easy to do, but life is certainly easier when we're not prickly and defensive.

I too remember being critical of my mom because I was a clueless teenager, struggling to develop an identity and feel good about myself. Mothers are often easy targets for displaced anger and fear. My daughters, in turn, said hurtful things to me at times. It helped to think of myself as a safety net, there to catch the negative thoughts and fears that were too difficult for my daughters to handle if they directed them inward.

No matter what our age, at times we have difficulty owning our problems and so we project our angst onto others. It's hard not to take disrespectful or unkind remarks personally, and we do need to stand up for ourselves so we don't become doormats. It's how we stand up for ourselves that's important. For example, as an educator, I remind myself that, "It's not all about me." That helps me remember not to take rude or harsh remarks from students personally and keeps me focused on my mission, which is teaching—not getting into petty arguments. I try to do the same thing in meetings and conversations. Keeping goals in mind helps me stay out of the thorny weeds and on the forgiveness path.

Forgiveness is a developmental construct. If we're fortunate, we get better at it. I asked Valerie how her concept of forgiveness had changed over time.

The Sin-Covering Eye

I have become much more tolerant of people. I made a lot of judgments when I was in my 20s and 30s, and thought people needed to change their views to fit mine. That really came back to bite me. We are all on our own paths to something better in life. We have free will and if we want people to respect our right to free will, we should respect their right as well. So when people do things I don't think are right or that I don't approve of, I try to have what the Baha'i faith calls a sin-covering eye."

"What does that mean?" I asked.

"For example, if a person has nine good qualities and one bad, ignore the bad one. If it's the other way around, nine bad qualities, one good, focus on the one good one and set aside the other nine."

"So focus on the positive and respect people's right to make mistakes?"

"Yes, exactly. I've made plenty of mistakes myself. And it's not the mistake that's important; it's how, once you realize you've made a mistake, you deal with it. How you change things. That's the important part."

Valerie differentiated a person's bad behavior from the person as an individual. "It's the act you don't have to accept in life, but you accept and forgive and love the person because they're still a human being. They're on their path."

Valerie's children are now adults and her son commented, "You're not raising us anymore so you don't have to contend with our problems." Her son was assuming life as a parent was easier with adult children. But Valerie smiled and told him, "Parenting goes beyond 18 years. Now you kids do things that worry me and I have absolutely no control."

"How do you practice forgiveness with your adult children?"

"I realize that I have weaknesses and so I try to recognize and focus on those weaknesses and work on them. My children are on their own path and I have to accept that they're smart and that tough experiences in life teach you things. I pray for them and hope they figure things out. I don't interfere too much because that just causes friction and I don't want to do that. I want to leave people in a peaceful state and show them I love them."

"So you accept and try to understand actions you may not agree with?"

"Yes. I try to keep peace so they can figure things out themselves. And I realize that I may be wrong in what I'm thinking. I admit I don't have all the answers."

Moral Identity: What Do You Want to Be When You Grow Up?

"What motivates you to forgive?" I asked Valerie.

"I decided at age 47 who I wanted to be when I grew up. I'm short and small so people often have thought I'm younger than I really am. For a long time I would get questions about who I wanted to be when I grew up. I never finished college and have never been good at finishing things. I knew I was pretty intelligent and had creative abilities, but I started really questioning who I was and what I wanted to be. I decided I wanted to be a nice, kind person. It doesn't make any difference what my skills or talents are, or whether I've completed something. I can use all my abilities to that end—to being kind—and that means being forgiving."

Valerie had a strong moral identity that guided her to forgiveness. She had no trouble choosing forgiveness. Forgiving described who she was and who she intended to keep being. She was willing to do the work and put forth the effort because it was something she believed in. Being kind and forgiving helped Valerie's mental and physical health.

"I have some physical health issues and they can make me a little depressed at times. So if there is an opportunity to do something good for somebody or to be more tolerant of somebody, then my depression goes away. When I'm working on my positive attitude I don't notice my symptoms as much. Healing is a two-part thing, material and spiritual. We are spiritual beings in a material body."

I asked Valerie what advice she had for people who are trying to forgive a major transgression. "Remember that we're all human and make mistakes. People need time to realize their mistake and figure out how to resolve it. They may not even know they hurt you. Accept the fact that people are at different levels of development and aren't necessarily aware of the pain they are causing others."

"And pray. Any prayer will do as long as it's sincere. Forgiveness is a necessary part of good spiritual, physical, and mental health. It's a positive action, whereas holding a grudge is a negative action and negative actions can impede your healing, your growth, and your happiness in life. It's just the right thing to do. God wants us to forgive."

"Why do you think God wants us to forgive?"

"Probably because it's good for us. I believe all of God's laws are for our benefit. We're here because God loves us. We're his children, his creation. God wants to direct us in the way that will be of the best benefit to us."

Valerie had a strong moral identity that valued forgiveness and she had supportive spiritual and religious connections that provided her with guidance. She had the courage to face difficult situations and conversations and her experiences had enhanced her ability to empathize and have compassion for others. Learning and spiritual growth were important to her and helped her create positive new chapters in her life story, a life that she felt would continue after her physical body had worn out.

Valerie felt forgiving others helped her be more forgiving of herself. Other persons I interviewed felt self-forgiveness was the first step toward forgiveness of others. What is the relationship between self-forgiveness and forgiveness of others or a situation? We will explore that in the next chapter.

DO I HAVE TO FORGIVE MYSELF IN ORDER TO FORGIVE OTHERS?

*Happiness is when what you think, what
you say, and what you do
are in harmony.*
—MAHATMA GANDHI

Forgiveness is meant to bring us peace of mind. To achieve peace of mind, what we think, do, and feel need to be in harmony. Can we harmonize if we are forgiving of ourselves, but not of others? Can we be in sync if we forgive others, but neglect doing the same for ourselves?

The majority of people I interviewed said that self-forgiveness facilitated forgiveness of others. They felt it created humility and empathy and explained that when they could accept and forgive themselves, they felt less threatened by others. Their identities were stronger and more secure, so they felt less like victims. The wall of blame and shame came down, so they were not afraid to take responsibility for any part they may have played in a misunderstanding or painful event. Self-forgiveness empowered them to be better problem solvers and innovators.

Katherine felt that confronting and forgiving a person's own faults and transgressions was needed to prevent defensive behavior that stymied forgiveness of others and personal growth. "I think you have to learn to forgive yourself first. That's the key. If you don't forgive yourself," Katherine explained, "you're always the bad guy. You try to cover it up, but you're always the bad guy. If you forgive yourself, you no longer feel threatened, and that makes you more expansive. You can forgive others. You stop saying, 'They did it to me,' and you say, 'Well, hey, what was my part in the equation?' You accept responsibility."

We all have some idea in our head of how we should be. We want to look good, smell good, make money, be respected, accomplish stuff, do things correctly, and be our own personal vision of perfection (since there is no global consensus on what that would mean). And some people seem to move forward towards their goals without much angst and chaos. Most of us, however, struggle at some time in our lives with maintaining good mental health and have moments of torment in which we "should" all over ourselves.

I should have done that.
I should not have said that.
I should be better at that.
I should not have eaten all of that.
I should have known better.
I should not have so much trouble being human.

Self-Compassion: What It Is and Is Not

To forgive ourselves we need to practice self-compassion, which involves accepting our failures, inadequacies, and regrets, and realizing hurt and pain is just part of being human. Self-compassion means having the courage to be open to our hurt, not avoiding or disconnecting from it, but inviting it in for coffee and a heart-to-heart chat. It means being aware of our thoughts, feelings, and past behaviors without over-identifying with them. We are *not* our negative thoughts and past regrets, and we can choose to change.

Self-compassion is different from self-pity. Self-pity can leave us feeling like helpless victims of unfair circumstances beyond our control. Self-compassion empowers us as we accept our frailties and failures and move forward with determination and loving kindness, aware that it's hard to be human, but confident we are up to the task.

Self-compassion is different from self-esteem in that it doesn't require any rewards, compliments, or high honors. We can just be our genuine selves. Self-esteem is based on an evaluation and, if overemphasized, can lead to an inflated sense of self and/or out-group prejudice. Self-compassion does not depend on outside appraisals. It listens to others while remembering that, ultimately, we determine our own identity. It opens our minds so we can realistically assess both our strengths and weaknesses. So we can better understand and accept ourselves just as we are.

Self-compassion is different than self-exoneration. Self-compassion means we take responsibility for our actions and work to better ourselves. Self-exoneration is about making excuses for our bad behavior or blaming others. It's about trying to escape responsibility, so we don't have to be the ones working on improving a situation or solving a problem.

If I'm feeling self-pity I may say, "Nothing ever seems to go my way. Either I'm messing up my life or someone else is." If I'm full of high self-esteem I may say, "I'm so glad I'm a member of the Glorious Group. We are real winners and I'm one of the most valuable people on the team." If I'm working toward self-exoneration I may say, "It's not my fault. Those other people should be punished and need to change." If I'm practicing self-compassion I say, "I sure wish I had done that differently, but thankfully I've learned a lot from the experience. I'll look for ways I can make amends for any damage I've done and try to help improve the situation."

Scrub Your Heart Clean

Esther and Ria talked about scrubbing their hearts clean as a first step in forgiveness of others. "You can say 'I forgive you,'" said Esther, "but it doesn't have any teeth until you know yourself, until you've worked. You've looked inside, you've seen who you are, and you've forgiven. You forgive yourself for being an imperfect human and scrub yourself clean. It's only then that you can forgive anyone else."

"Until I could forgive myself," William stated, "there was no way I could forgive anybody else. I had to identify the source of my negative feelings and what it was that I chose to feel anger or hurt or pain for." Self-forgiveness allowed William to take responsibility for his feelings and deal with them constructively.

Self, other, and situation forgiveness are interwoven and all have as their foundation an acceptance of what we see as the deficiencies and injustices of life—the messiness of our human condition. Forgiveness is facilitated when we recognize our common humanity and the difficulties we all face making good choices and controlling our not-so-nice impulses.

People I interviewed often described unforgiveness as a personal prison and forgiveness as freedom. "To forgive is to set a prisoner free and discover that the prisoner was you," said Lewes B. Smedes, renowned Christian author, ethicist, and theologian.

I know it's easy for me to become imprisoned by negative ruminations—destructive thoughts that keep repeating themselves. When that happens, I may slip into blaming others or feeling debilitating shame for the ways I messed up or failed. I get on my pity potty or spend time on my treadmill going nowhere. Pain and hurt block my view of the beauty in life as well as the needs of others. I'm not solving any problems, my burden is heavy, and my vision is obstructed by clouds of self-pity or self-righteous indignation.

That's when I know I need to break free and take flight. I start thinking about what good things I can do for others, which gets my mind off my problems and makes me feel better about myself. I read, listen, reflect, and open my mind to new viewpoints while trying to put my sorrows in perspective.

Forgiving Ourselves Means Taking Responsibility

Can forgiving yourself be a bad thing? Fadel insisted it was important that he *not* forgive himself. I did some probing to better comprehend what he meant by that. The more Fadel and I talked, the more I felt what he meant was he did not want to self-excuse or exonerate himself.

Fadel had two reasons why he felt *not* forgiving (or excusing) himself was important. The first was that he felt being aware of his weaknesses and taking responsibility for his mistakes helped him improve himself and be a better person. "I do accept and confront my mistakes," he said, "but I will not forgive myself for doing the mistake. It helps me to be more aware. I am responsible for my actions and hold myself fully accountable. I want to reach higher levels and push myself to be better."

The second reason Fadel felt he should not forgive himself was so that he could better forgive others. Remaining aware of and accountable for his own offenses increased his humility and kept his pride in check. "It's good to be aware of who you are and remember you make mistakes. When I remember my own mistakes, I am better able to forgive others because I realize I am not better than them."

Fadel's non-self-forgiveness goals were the same as other persons' self-forgiveness goals. Everyone I interviewed wanted to learn, grow, and better themselves, as well as have more empathy and humility so they could better forgive others. They wanted to take responsibility for their behaviors and welcomed the challenge of self-improvement.

Is it more difficult to forgive oneself than others? The majority of people I interviewed said yes. They had higher expectations for themselves and were more critical of themselves than of others.

Many of us grew up in an environment in which we were chastised for not performing well and we still struggle with those negative voices that intrude into our thoughts and nourish our shame. Our brains are structured to enhance our chances of survival, so it's natural that our focus is often on the negatives we need to correct rather than the positives that are fine just as they are. The key is not letting the negative voices lock you in a personal prison of despair.

Mommy Guilt

Valerie felt self-forgiveness was more difficult than forgiveness of others and experienced what is sometimes called "Mommy guilt"—something that is a struggle for many women. Dads can certainly experience regrets as well. Parenting is a difficult job that often perplexes and challenges us.

Valerie explained one of her parenting regrets. "I'm a smoker and I didn't quit when I was pregnant with my children. I know that some of their health problems are probably due to that. But with my first two pregnancies, smoking was not seen as harmful. I still feel bad though, especially since one of my children has Parkinson's disease and it may be connected."

"How do you deal with guilt?" I asked.

"I know I shouldn't beat myself up too badly about what happened in the past because I can't go back and do it over. But

I can and do apologize. The 12-step program for alcoholics is a good model for self-forgiveness. First, you find something larger than yourself to believe in. Then you confront the hurtful things you've done and try to make amends for them.'"

"For example," explained Valerie, "I was working a lot when my kids were young and I gave my oldest daughter lots of responsibility and made her babysit a lot. She finally exploded at me and reminded me, 'They're your kids, Mom, not mine.' I realized she was right and I apologized. But still to this day, guilt creeps back a little bit, even though I've tried very hard to forgive myself. It especially comes back if I see my kids struggling with something that maybe I had an influence on. But I remind myself I cannot rewrite history. I can just apologize and make amends as best I can. I use prayer for self-forgiveness too."

Valerie felt the more you forgive other people the more you can forgive yourself. Forgiving others made her feel good about herself and helped her keep true to her moral identity. This in turn helped her feel more compassion toward herself. She had regrets, but realized everyone did. She knew that even though she'd behaved badly at times, she'd also been kind, loving, and a positive influence.

Self-forgiveness is aided if we are fortunate enough to grow up in an environment that provides unconditional love and positive regard. But even if we do, certain things will be very difficult to forgive—such as feeling responsible for the loss of a child. Rose shared an experience that occurred before her family members' murders and that helped her grow in forgiveness. The story involved the birth of her first son.

"Our first son died in my arms when he was only half-an-hour old. He was born prematurely and had serious medical problems—his intestines were located outside his stomach. When I was carrying my son I felt something was not right, but I didn't want to go to the doctor because I was afraid of being given bad news. However, after I had the baby, I regretted not getting better health care. I had to learn to forgive myself for that."

"How were you able to do that?" I asked.

"Through prayer and feeling his spirit. We named him and buried him in our family plot. In prayer circles and in Lakota ceremonies people have seen his spirit standing beside me, tall and handsome with long hair. One side is loose and one side is gathered into a braid."

Rose learned to let go of her guilt, but losing her son was very hard. "I couldn't eat regularly for about a month because every time I took a bite of food I'd think of my son, who couldn't eat because he was dead. I equated food with life. I had to do a lot of praying about that. I still have to pray hard around the dates my son died and my mother and sister died. I use my Sacred Pipe to pray and stay connected to them. I thank the Creator for their lives."

Reach Out

Tough forgiveness events like the death of a child prompt us to reach out to something beyond ourselves. I've heard people call that something many names. There are the typical words like God, Allah, Holy Spirit, and Jesus as well as the less typical, but no less authentic, words like Universe, Divine Feminine, Source, Angels, and Wakan Tanka (the Great Mystery). The important thing is that the name, symbol, or visual represents love and light to you and that it aids your healing and growth.

The "Course in Miracles," a curriculum published by the Foundation for Inner Peace, has led some people to forgiveness. It asks us to choose between a grievance and a miracle, and emphasizes embracing the loving spirit that lives within us as we move towards forgiveness. It asks whether we want to view the world as a classroom or as a battleground.

All the major religions profess a belief in the oneness of God and the connection we all have with one another. If I hurt you, I also hurt me. If I hurt myself, my hurt spreads to all those who love me. When we feel a connectedness to others and to the divine, lines of separation melt and forgiveness flows more freely.

What does it mean to be one with God? I wonder if oneness with God or the universe works on a grand scale in a way that is similar to how our individual bodies work on a small scale. When I study biopsychology, I am in awe of the power and sentience of our neurons (brain cells) as well as the other microscopic units of life in our bodies. Scientists estimate we have up to 100 trillion cells in our bodies. What's amazing to me is that each cell is a teeny, tiny decider that affects the other microscopic deciders. Their communication and ability to work together ultimately affects our body as a whole. The more healthy cells we have in our body, the more likely we are to grow strong and resistant to disease and injury. Every cell is important to the body as a whole.

Forgiveness Contributes to the Health of the World

Forgiveness is about healing and growth. When we heal, it enables others to heal as well. As an offense is transformed from a stab wound into a battle scar of courage and progress, guilt and bitterness melt away. Forgiveness allows us to shine the light of love on others and do our part in nourishing positive relationships and communities. It's our contribution to the health of the world.

Our next forgiveness hero, Ben, was able to overcome the guilt he felt because of the part he played in a tragic accident resulting in the death of a young husband and father. He was able to forgive himself, which allowed him to use the courage, compassion, and wisdom he gained from the tragedy to help others and improve safety at his workplace.

GIVE YOURSELF TIME: BEN'S STORY OF SELF-FORGIVENESS

Even a happy life cannot be without a measure of darkness,
and the word happy would lose its meaning
if it were not balanced by sadness.
It is far better to take things as they come
along with patience and equanimity.

—CARL JUNG

Self-forgiveness can be especially difficult. We can't escape from ourselves and if we try to, the result can be fatal. Turning to alcohol or other mind-altering substances, addictions of various kinds, severe depression, suicide, all indicate failed attempts at self-forgiveness. As Carl Jung noted, being human means we encounter moments of light and of darkness. When those dark times come, we need courage and compassion so we can create meaning, so we can understand and accept the hard times that feel so painful and hopeless.

The tougher the times, the more patience and resilience it will take to persevere and transform tragedy into triumph. It took our next forgiveness hero, Ben, one and a half years to lighten his burden of guilt, shame, and anger.

I interviewed Ben two days before he was ready to celebrate his thirty-sixth birthday. Ben was a well-loved husband and father and a caring Christian youth pastor who'd grown up in Texas and spent ten years in the US Air Force. He had a big truck, a big heart, and a positive attitude toward life and people. But Ben's life could have been much different if he hadn't been able to forgive himself for an incident that happened when he was eighteen years old. "My life would have been so much darker if I hadn't been able to forgive myself," he reflected.

Ben explained to me the tragic accident that ended in the death of the senior airman who was one rank above him and who was a husband and father of two young children. The Senior Airman, Steve, was training Ben and Justin, both Airmen First Class, on how to troubleshoot and diagnose problems with a generator. Ben and Justin were electrical power production apprentices at the time and had recently finished basic training and tech school.

"Steve, Justin, and I were going through the troubleshooting process of figuring out what was wrong with a generator that was not functioning correctly," explained Ben. "We determined the fuel pump was not operating properly so we took the fuel pump off and sent it in to be rebuilt. That meant we had to take the fan shroud off the generator and that exposed the steel fan blades."

"Several days later we got the fuel pump back and needed to reinstall it to get everything working again. There were gears and timing lines that had to be set up correctly and tested so fuel could be sent to the engine. The front of the gears is in the same area as the fan blade for the engine. The shrouding goes over the fan blades."

Taking the shrouding off and on the fan blades would take time, and Ben knew they may have to do some retiming and several tests before the generator was running properly again. He suggested they leave the fan shroud off in case they needed to pull everything back apart and do some retiming. That seemed more efficient. Steve agreed, as did Justin. The decision was made and the three men turned their focus to the tests they needed to perform.

"Steve found a missing cylinder that wasn't firing correctly," said Ben. "He asked me to come over to where he was at so he could show me how to fix the problem."

It was a warm day in June and the three men were in a room with a generator running. They were hot and it didn't help that they needed to wear coveralls to protect their uniforms. Steve had decided to lessen his discomfort by taking his coveralls down to his waist, flipping his sleeves over, and tying them in a knot. This turned out to be a deadly decision.

"Steve was standing on a concrete pad and needed to slide down in order for me to listen to and understand what he'd found out about the cylinder that was misfiring," said Ben. "When he did, he slid down close enough to the fan blade opening that the sleeve he had tied around his waist got pulled into the steel fan blades. When that happened, it pulled him in along with it. It moved him down and pulled him into an extremely small opening. Those motors and engines aren't little, they're big, and it didn't even bog down. It didn't even stop. It just pulled him in and kept going."

Ben and Justin were stunned by the horrific sight before them. "It seemed to us, and I know it wasn't, but it seemed like an eternity from when it dawned on us what had happened to when we stopped the motor. We hit the emergency stop and Steve basically folded in half and kind of slumped over. We freaked out, but still realized we needed a radio; we needed to call for help. We ran out of the building trying to get on the radio and ran into some airmen just returning from lunch. They realized we needed assistance and helped take over. I got on the radio but didn't realize all I was doing was yelling. I was terrified and wasn't properly operating the radio, so no one could figure out what was going on."

Other airmen stepped in and directed Ben and Justin to the fire department building which was right next door. Fellow airmen took charge of the situation which had left Ben and Justin in shock. They determined what had happened and were later able to explain to the young airmen that their senior officer, Steve, would have died instantly.

The horrible incident changed Ben's life. Not only did he have to live with the trauma of watching the dreadful death of his senior officer, a young husband and father who was just beginning his career. Ben also had to deal with guilt, as he felt responsible for the accident.

"It was my idea to leave the fan shroud off just to save time," remembered Ben. "I struggled with that for a long time. I still do every now and then when I think about it. I understand I was a young airman and I didn't know any better. I know all three of us played a part in the decision and ultimately it was up to the senior airman. I know the circumstances just played out in that particular way. But it took me about a year and a half to come to terms with my part in the incident, and to realize it wasn't all my fault."

Post-Traumatic Stress

Witnessing Steve's death was traumatic and stressful. The Air Force recognized the harmful consequences of post-traumatic stress and put actions in place to help Ben recover from his experience. He was able to continue working at the air base for six more years. "What made that possible?" I asked.

"I never had to work on the piece of equipment that took Steve's life again," Ben responded. "I didn't even have to go into the facility where the accident happened except one time after that."

Post-Traumatic Stress Disorder (PTSD) is conceptualized as a fear-based disorder. Returning to the facility or the equipment could have triggered painful memories and easily produced an anxious, fearful response. Ben had to process his experience, but there was no need to make that process more difficult by exposing him to stimuli that could ignite flashbacks and flood him with dark thoughts and visions.

"Witnessing the horrific event was very hard" Ben said, "but the forgiveness process was harder. I blamed myself for a lot of the decisions that happened that day. I took full ownership of what happened and it weighed heavy on me. It was my idea that we decided upon. It was going to save us some time and it ended up taking a life."

Moral Injury

In addition to the stress of observing a traumatic event, Ben was experiencing something that could be called a moral injury. A moral injury is determined by how an individual evaluates an event. Does the event generate cognitive dissonance by causing significant discord between what happened and what the individual believed should have happened? And does that discord involve morals, trust, and spiritual/existential issues?

Treatment for PTSD focuses on lessening the fear response and reducing anxiety. Treatment for moral injury is about trying to make sense of an event that we morally believe shouldn't have happened; that disturbs our worldview as well as our view of ourselves as individuals.[26] Recovering from a moral injury requires forgiveness.

Ben was mad at himself and struggled with guilt. Even though we know bad things happen to good people, it's hard to imagine that those bad things will actually happen to us until they do. Ben's fellow airman had died and so had Ben's youthful idealism. Things like horrifying accidental deaths are not supposed to happen and we certainly aren't supposed to contribute to them happening in any way. We grieve for the people who are gone and we grieve for our old self. The self we had imagined would never experience whatever it is that is rocking our world, keeping us up at night, confusing and tormenting us. The self that wouldn't make mistakes that lead to tragic results.

Ben was also angry at God. "Up until that point nothing really bad had happened to me. When that terrible accident occurred, I was extremely mad and spent time away from God," said Ben. "I asked, 'God, how could you allow this to happen? Why did all this have to happen? Why do I have to go through all this? Why does Steve's family have to go through this?' A lot of why questions. I spent a lot of time really mad at God."

"How did your questions get answered?"

"I think it was just gradual," Ben responded. "Counseling definitely helped. Justin and I both had free access to counselors anytime we needed them. For six months I had appointments set up weekly that I had to go to."

"What about the counseling made it helpful?" I asked.

"I could talk freely about all of it. Out loud I could talk about my emotions and what I was feeling. I'd never seen anything remotely so traumatic and horrific in my life and I needed to talk about it. Also, they reminded me that Steve's death was not my fault. Multiple things happened that day that caused the accident. It wasn't just leaving the fan shroud off. I was able to forgive myself knowing that it wasn't directly my fault."

"How were you able to get over your anger with God?" I wondered.

"I gradually became able to accept the situation and what had happened. That the world is not necessarily rainbows and ice-cream and fluffy fun things. There's traumatic events and there's struggles in life. That's part of life. Once I could accept what had happened and quit blaming myself, I realized God is with us through good times and bad times, no matter what. There is an unconditional love from God. God is still with us, caring for us, when we are hurt and in pain."

Guilt and Shame

Guilt and shame can overwhelm us. They are powerful emotions. We wish we could go back and get a do-over. We want to make different choices in the past, but the choices we have to make are for the future. Will we learn to forgive, grow, move forward; or will we choose to remain trapped in reruns of dark shadows and painful regrets?

Guilt and shame are related but different. Guilt is about realizing, "I did something bad." It's about having the courage to face what we've done, about taking responsibility and feeling remorse. If we can learn from our mistakes and atone for whatever we have done, self-forgiveness will generally follow.

Shame is feeling, "I am bad." It's related to how we believe we are perceived by others as well as how we perceive ourselves. If others dishonor, disrespect, humiliate us, it is hard to maintain a positive view of who we are. We may decide we are entirely bad and lose hope for a better future. Shame can hinder forgiveness because we don't feel worthy of compassion and, because of our negative assessment of ourselves, we are blind to opportunities for improvement and redemption.

Ben was fortunate in that his employer, the US Air Force, as well as his wife and close friends, never shamed him. They didn't dismiss Ben's part in the tragedy, but instead supported him as he struggled with his thoughts and feelings, which he transformed through courage, compassion, and creativity. "The incident could easily have derailed my whole life if I hadn't had the relationship with the people I did and with God," Ben reflected.

Supportive Connections

"How did your wife support you?" I inquired.

"I relied a lot on my wife," remembered Ben. "We'd just been married a few months at that time and were away from our families. My wife was always there. There were a lot of times, especially right after the accident, when I didn't want to go places by myself. I didn't want to be alone, especially in the dark. There were a lot of emotions going on at the time, and she was always there. She was there when I was struggling with what I saw and what I was feeling. That was meaningful. To have had people

who were willing to just be there, willing to listen and be physically present."

"It sounds like you were able to receive unconditional support and love from the important people in your life," I reflected.

"Yes. They gave me space to work through the incident and
were always there for me. That seems like kind of a weird way
of saying it—maybe contradictory—but that's the way it was.
They didn't pressure me. They listened and allowed me to work
through what I needed to work through according to my own
timetable."

Ben was fortunate. Forgiveness can feel like a burden if it's
forced or rushed. For some people, being told they do *not* need
to forgive may actually help them forgive. We may need to feel
free of the expectations of others so we can genuinely explore
and grapple with whatever is going on in our minds. So we can
find our own path to peace and well-being. Some people want
to just let God do the forgiving, or simply not worry about what
they have been told they *should* be feeling or doing.[27]

Ben's coworker, Justin, was not able to mentally overcome the
tragedy and had to be medically separated from the Air Force.
I asked Ben what gave him the strength to forgive himself and
continue on for six more years of service.

"I grew up going to church regularly in Texas. My faith and
religion were always a part of me. I spent a lot of time angry with
God after the incident, but even in the midst of that I still knew
I needed God and needed to rely on Him. I reached out right
away to the pastor of our church and his wife. We were new in

town and weren't even members of the church yet, but I knew I needed spiritual help."

God is sometimes referred to as a parent who gives unconditional love and mercy. Ben had established a firm religious foundation and could rage at God in much the same way a teenager quarrels with a parent she or he does not yet understand. With time, Ben's disputes with God led to a more mature spiritual relationship.

Transforming Pain into Purpose

With time, Ben was able to view the tragic event in a different light. "I came to realize that there could be a purpose, a reason, for painful things that happen. The experience has made me a stronger person. The incident was just a piece of time, not my whole life. It was important I didn't make it my whole life."

Ben shared one of his favorite Bible verses, Ephesians 2:10, which says "We are God's handiwork, created in Christ Jesus to do good works, which God prepared in advance for us to do." (New International Version). "That verse helps me to know we're each created in a unique way for a purpose," explained Ben. "It reminds me that the stuff I've gone through, the path my life has taken, was for a particular reason. I didn't just stumble upon where I'm at today. Everything was put in motion for a reason. It's God's handiwork to get us where we're at. We may not always like the journey we have to take, the path we have to take to get there. But there are reasons and there's purpose for it."

Helen Keller noted, "We could never learn to be brave and patient if there was only joy in the world." Ben learned to be brave and patient and realized his experience had sculpted him into the person he had become. A person who was able to work with youth and young adults and help them feel loved and cared for. Ben realized the tragic incident had created a new and improved Ben who could listen, empathize, and generously pass along the compassion and grace he had received.

The accident also prompted global Air Force safety improvements in electrical power production operating procedures and equipment design. "I was able to use my experience to help in training others and I contributed to a safer, improved system," said Ben. "I went to different training events across the Air Force and had the opportunity to explain what happened and explain how to prevent something like that from happening again. The accident led to positive changes. That helped me work through things and I could start viewing the accident not just as a horrible human tragedy, but also as the impetus for creating a safer electrical generator system worldwide. Promoting safety features for the future helped me atone for what happened."

Impediments to Forgiveness

Ben learned a lot about courage and compassion on his forgiveness journey and created a healthy path forward. But being human is hard and new challenges keep coming our way. I asked Ben to describe his greatest impediments to forgiveness.

"My own stubbornness. Being stubborn and human have got to be the biggest things for me. That and sometimes not slowing down enough to think things through. To think about how and why someone is acting the way they are—myself included."

"What have you learned to do when people disappoint or hurt you, or you are disappointed in yourself?" I asked.

"I work at being more compassionate and try to look beneath the surface for the reasons why someone is lashing out or being aggravating. Being in the military, we moved a lot and had to change jobs. It's hard to leave close friends and coworkers and that can create sadness and fear that's disguised as anger. I try to look for underlying causes for offensive behavior and show more compassion for whatever circumstances are creating the hurtful actions. I've learned to give more grace and less judgment."

Judgment without mercy and compassion creates problems in our relationships, and may create especially difficult problems in our relationship with ourselves. I asked Ben to describe his experience with forgiveness of self and others.

"Sometimes it's so much easier to forgive others. For example, with the accident, I didn't place any guilt on my senior airman for the whole situation. I tried to shoulder it all myself, to carry the full burden. It took time to develop an understanding that all three of us played a part in the circumstances that happened. My expectations for myself were way too high. We expect more perfection from ourselves than we're able to achieve. We have to admit we make mistakes and are always learning and growing."

"Has forgiving yourself helped you forgive others?" I asked.

"Yes, I think so. I took responsibility for the part I played in the accident and accepted forgiveness for my errors and for being human. That opened a door for me and created more room for forgiveness of others. I'm more able to empathize and realize that people may be going through emotions similar to what I have gone through. What's on the surface often isn't the whole story. I learned the importance of grace and forgiveness."

There's no better teacher than experience. All of our senses are involved, as are our thoughts, feelings, and behaviors. We are truly all in. The next best teacher is a story that transports you into the world of another, challenges your thinking, and engages your heart. That's how we gain empathy.

Work Through It in Your Own Time

I asked Ben the question that I asked all the forgiveness heroes I interviewed. "What's your advice to others who are deciding whether to choose forgiveness or who are working through the process?"

"Definitely work through it in your own time. That's a gift that I was given. The time to do it. Don't rush things. Work through all those painful, confusing feelings and emotions. Then, when the time is right for you and you feel able—forgive. Forgive whoever you're angry with. Especially if it's yourself. But an important thing I learned from my experience was that you've got to be ready to forgive."

Forgiving a transgression that has had a major impact on you is a growth experience. That's why it takes time and that's also why it changes your life.

Unleash Your Thoughts and Feelings

The process of forgiving requires communication. Communication is how we figure things out. We can talk to our higher power or spirit guide; to supportive people; to the people whom we need to forgive—living or dead; to the people whom we'd like to forgive us—living or dead. We can communicate out loud by speaking or through writing. We can receive guidance by listening and reading. The important thing is dialoguing in some way with our supportive connections and whoever it is we need to resolve things with.

Ben was mad at God and he was mad at himself. He was also upset with Steve. If only Steve hadn't gone along with his idea to leave the fan shroud off. If only he hadn't tied his coverall sleeve around his waist. If only he'd been more careful when sliding down to show Ben what to do.

Ben needed to talk to Steve about his feelings, to share his thoughts with him. Steve was buried in a cemetery not far from Ben's home, so that's the place where the needed conversations were able to take place.

"Especially right after the incident happened, I would go to the cemetery and talk to Steve," explained Ben. "I forgave Steve for what happened and I asked him to forgive me for the things I did that led to the event. It was helpful and healthy for me to do so. I was able to openly express my feelings, not keep them bottled up inside. There's something about putting it out there, getting it out of your head, vocalizing it or writing it down. It helped once what was inside me was out and I could hear it."

Our dark thoughts lose power over us when we express them. They become less scary. Once we uncover them we can start taming them. They leave their cave and are exposed to light. They can be transformed from demons that control us into naughty youngsters that we need to discipline now and then.

Forgiveness Makes Growth Possible

Ben described what the word forgiveness meant to him. "Coming to terms with whatever has happened to hurt us and whatever part we played in it, and being okay enough with that to move on and to grow."

Once we've reached an understanding of the painful event and done whatever work we needed to do to feel okay about it, our pain recedes and no longer has the power to damage us. We don't forget painful offenses, but we remember them differently when we forgive. The memories may sadden us and still have the power to cause tears to fall, but they no longer haunt us. They become lessons that move us forward with more compassion, courage, and creativity than we had before.

Ben became slightly tearful when talking about remembering Steve, not because he was upset, but because his heart was full and spilling over. "I don't ever want to forget what happened. And that seems weird to say, but it keeps his memory alive. It keeps me grounded and humble. Forgiving is not forgetting. It's being willing to grow and be okay with whatever happened."

We hurt when we do something we believe is unforgiveable, and that pain can be fatal if we don't believe we are worthy of forgiveness. We need to be strong enough to forgive ourselves so we can pass the gift of forgiveness on to others, as Ben was able to do. Ben took the time to grapple with his genuine feelings and communicate his painful thoughts with others. He created a positive path forward by taking responsibility for his mistakes without hurting himself or others in the process. His courage and compassion allowed him to accept grace and practice forgiveness.

"God does forgive," said Ben, "and there are no limits. We are allowed whatever space and room we need to grow. God gives us grace and we can pass that on to others. We all need grace."

Grace cleanses us, empowers us, and gives us hope. Compassion and courage light our path as we create a new and improved chapter in our life story. The next chapters provide guidance from our forgiveness heroes as to ways to create a brighter future.

CREATE A NEW CHAPTER IN YOUR LIFE STORY

Creativity is the greatest expression of liberty.
—BRYANT H. MCGILL

Creativity is sometimes uncreatively thought of as innate artistic ability, limited to crafts and museum pieces, and divorced from hard work and persistence. But that is an inadequate, unimaginative way of thinking about it.

Creativity is what liberates us from old ideas that are no longer working or that need updates. Creativity drives us to generate new stories. It is effortful and requires perseverance. But it is oh so exciting and satisfying to travel to a new and improved destination on the road of life.

So how will we define creativity? First, creativity will mean a mind open to new ideas, unrestricted in its application. A fortune cookie told me, "If you never change your mind, why have one?" Sometimes we get very stubborn about our views and tenaciously cling to ideas we've constructed about how certain things and people ought to be. But our minds are made for learning and adapting, no matter what age we are.

Second, creativity will mean gritty determination and persistence in finding new and better solutions to problems. Creative people work hard to produce something new because they do not shrink from a challenge and appreciate the benefits of positive change. Remember Thomas Edison's famous words describing his unsuccessful attempts at creating the first light bulb. He said, "I have not failed. I've just found 10,000 ways that won't work."

Forgiving a major offense requires creativity, because we will naturally feel hurt, disappointed, and thrown off guard when our life takes a turn it's not supposed to take. We ask ourselves questions such as the following:

How could she cheat and deceive me?
Why did this horrible catastrophe happen to me?
How could I have been so stupid and mean?
Why does he continue to abuse me?

An offense is offensive because it was not supposed to happen. But unfortunately it did, and perhaps it's still happening.

What's next? Once you've uncovered and understood your pain, it's time to create a new story in which you are the hero, not the victim. You become the person to be admired, not the person to be pitied. Our suffering and pain leads us to the conclusion that, "There's got to be another way—a better way to handle this."

Jacob, our next forgiveness hero, created a better way of thinking and being when his spiritual journey took him from atheism and agnosticism back to Judaism where he began. He began meditating and chanting, becoming more aware of the need to control his anger and rage and make responsible choices. He still prays, "Oh God, help me live with my imperfections."

BECOMING AWARE OF MY CHOICES: JACOB'S STORY

Creativity requires the courage to let go of certainties.
—ERICH FROMM

When I first reached out to Jacob, he warned me that his story of forgiveness may not be as ideal as I would like. "I'm not sure I have ever really completely forgiven anyone for anything serious," he warned me. "But I work at it. A lot. And I use Jewish practice to inform my attempts."

Forgiveness can be messy. Truly and completely forgiving a painful offense is very hard. We need to forgive ourselves for not being perfect forgivers. Even when we think we've forgiven, a tone of voice or suspicious look may ignite our defensive shield. A memory we thought we had under control surfaces and we find ourselves feeling tormented once more. A stressful day sets off an angry tantrum as our self-discipline melts.

Jacob's heritage was Judaism, but he had 'converted' to atheism in junior high, moved on to agnosticism, and then headed back to Judaism in his thirties when he became consciously aware of his spiritual self. His practice of Judaism was deepened and transformed when he read *The Jew in the Lotus*, a 1994 book by Rodger Kamenetz about a historic dialogue between rabbis and the Dalai Lama. He took up meditating and chanting and started appreciating the mystical practices of Judaism.

Do Forgiveness, Don't Just Believe in It

"Judaism is a practice more than a belief system," Jacob stated. "You don't have to believe in God, just act like you believe in God."

Jacob was a lawyer and very aware that words could be interpreted in different ways. "I'm interested in the meaning and actions behind the words expressed as beliefs," he explained.

Jacob's imperfect story of forgiveness involved a painful misunderstanding between himself and the executive director (ED) of a nonprofit organization. Jacob served as chair of the board of directors. The Board had hired a full-time ED, but later discovered that their financial status was not strong enough to sustain her employment at that level.

Jacob had maintained a positive, trusting relationship with the ED, whom we'll call Susan, up to the point of the misunderstanding. Susan realized the organization had to face their financial problems and that her salary comprised a large percentage of the budget, but she was naturally worried about her own financial situation. Jacob was the lead negotiator, the go-between, for the Board. "The ED trusted me and I her at that time. She asked me to take her requests for contract changes to the Board for her, which I did."

Communication over sensitive issues such as money is always challenging and this situation proved to be no exception. Jacob explained Susan's proposal to his fellow board members and they spent several hours discussing what revisions to her contract they were and were not willing to grant. An offer was sent to Susan by email.

Email messages lack non-verbal cues and don't provide the opportunity for clear discourse. They can be ripe for misinterpretation and assumptions, especially if the matter presented ignites our defensive emotions. As may have been predicted, misunderstandings occurred. It reached a point where Jacob felt it best that he step back from his role as person-to-person negotiator.

"How did that make you feel?" I asked Jacob.

"I was shocked and disappointed by Susan's response to my well intentioned efforts. It made me angry."

Misunderstandings and Broken Communication
Lead to Disappointment, Hurt, and Anger

It is especially disappointing and painful when we have expended time and energy to do our best and assume we have acted appropriately, only to discover that the reaction to our efforts is entirely different than what we had anticipated. If the negative reaction is coming from someone we've trusted and been close to, we may feel betrayed and grieve the loss of a valued relationship.

Ineffective negotiations between the Board and Susan continued for several months, and then Jacob received another shock. Susan hired a lawyer. People often hire lawyers with the expectation that the lawyer can better represent them than they would be able to do themselves. Sometimes people are tired of trying to reach a solution themselves and so want to hand off to someone they think will help them meet their goal. Managing conflict is challenging, and for most people, no fun.

Jacob explained that it had been his experience as a lawyer that getting someone in his profession involved often makes things more difficult to resolve, not easier. He related a story that reflected his thoughts. "When a town has one lawyer, that lawyer will starve; when a second lawyer arrives in town, both will do very well. Without lawyers, people work things out; with lawyers, they fight things out."

Hiring a lawyer had the effect of elevating the disagreement between Susan and the Board to a new level. And, as with the previous emails, the words of the letter, as well as the act of hiring an attorney, left plenty of room for assumptions and misinterpretation.

"The email from the lawyer felt like an ultimatum," said Jacob, "both because of the content and tone of the message, and because Susan's message came from her attorney, not from her personally. It felt like a breaking off of relations—in effect, a declaration of war. It did not read like a negotiation or a discussion."

The entrance of Susan's lawyer complicated matters further because the code of ethics for lawyers prohibits contact with another lawyer's client without permission from the other lawyer. Jacob and several other board members were lawyers, so they asked Susan's lawyer if they could communicate with her directly. Susan's lawyer said no. The Board did not want to continue direct communication with Susan without the participation of all board members; therefore, dialogue between the Board and Susan herself came to a standstill.

Jacob explained that the Board had hoped to keep their long-term relationship with Susan intact. "We didn't want to terminate Susan's employment, but we did need her to step away from full-time employment until we could hopefully raise the money needed to support that. The lawyer's letter, however, made us feel like we had no choice but to terminate her prior contract. Consequently, we did so."

Communication with the ED was very important, and so was communicating what was happening to the membership of the organization. However, confidentiality rules regarding personnel issues meant the Board could not explain to the membership what was happening. With opportunities for dialogue ending, new problems began.

"Susan sent an email to the membership stating she went on unpaid leave to keep the organization alive, and had hoped to hear from the Board about a long-term relationship. She said the Board did not reach out to her. She stated she did not believe the Board acted in bad faith or with malice, and she stated there were misunderstandings on both sides."

"How did that make you feel?"

"Even though Susan's email said all the right words, I felt it presented a 'good guys versus bad guys' narrative and that I and the Board were the bad guys. The perception of the membership was that we had treated the ED badly, running her off, publicly humiliating her. I was depicted as the ringleader. The atmosphere became poisonous, but the Board felt legally obligated to remain silent."

When people don't know what's going on they devise their own scenarios. When it feels like there are secrets or schemes people become fearful and defensive. Trust is scarce and genuine feelings may be repressed. "People felt like they were walking on eggshells and that someone would be offended if what they said was not just right," Jacob noted. "We argued over whether a table should be square or round in order to avoid talking about what really mattered."

Prevent Wounded Feelings from Erupting

Jacob was concerned for the organization, and he was worried about himself. "I worried my wounded feelings would erupt, possibly at the worst possible moment, in a destructive manner. I knew I needed to do something. Jewish holidays that encouraged forgiveness work were approaching. I asked myself, 'If I don't do something now, when?'"

A teaching from Hillel the Elder, leader of the Jewish Supreme Court in the Land of Israel in the early part of the 1st Century CE. (Pirkei Avot, Chapter 1:14) guided Jacob's decision to devote time to forgiving and not wait.

If I am not for myself, who will be for me?
If I am only for myself, what am I?
And if not now, when?

Jacob realized that repressing our fears and true feelings buries them temporarily, but like resilient weeds, they will find a way to surface and grow. Uncovering the roots of our problems and figuring out how to deal with them prevents anger and hate from insidiously growing inside us.

In the Jewish tradition, the High Holy Days of Rosh Hashanah (Head of the Year) and Yom Kippur (Day of Atonement) and the ten days between them are a time of reflection upon the missteps of the past year and inner work to change oneself so as to do better in the coming year. Jacob described the scripture surrounding the High Holy Days. "On Rosh Hashanah, God is said to write your fate for the next year in the Book of Life. But in the next ten days, you have an opportunity to make corrections, to turn in a new direction, and by doing so persuade God to change what is written. On Yom Kippur God decides upon the final writing, and closes and seals the Book of Life for the coming year."

Jacob explained he takes the prescriptions for the High Holy Days as metaphors that provide him with useful guidance on how to live. "Years ago, I decided to use the Jewish High Holy Days to work hard on a relationship I wanted to improve. I knew it was time for me to work on my relationship with Susan."

"How did you do that?" I questioned.

"Every day I spent time dealing with my anger, my hurt, my damaged dignity, and my self-importance. I tried to gain perspective and found out how to constructively deal with my feelings. I decided to write Susan a long letter describing my actions and the Board's actions as I perceived them. I rewrote the letter many times and probably spent up to forty hours writing it, which didn't count all the time I spent thinking about writing it."

Don't Let Anger Use You: Transform Anger into Useful Energy

"What made writing the letter effective?"

"I didn't want my feelings to control me anymore because I knew that wasn't good for me, and it wasn't good for the organization. When writing the letter, I tried to be objective and worked to detach from the situation so I could see it more clearly. I rewrote the letter many times, each time trying to take the blame and anger out of the letter. The letter was about my feelings and perceptions. I was uncovering and confronting them. I wanted my feelings to help me better understand the situation, instead of letting my feelings use me."

"How did you feel after you put the letter in the mail?"

"Done. I felt closure, free. Anger has been a part of my life and it has used me. I get angry at injustice and can feel rage, which is an emotion that has the power to control me. So I try to work on it, sit with it, and transform it into something useful. Anger can fuel me, push me to fight for justice. But it can also hurt me if I don't control it."

Thinking back, Jacob realized, "The exercise and discipline of taking the anger out of the words of the letter took the anger out of me."

"Did you receive a response back from Susan?" I asked.

"No, and that caused me to lose some respect for her. I do not feel able to trust her, though I don't feel vulnerable, as she no longer has the ability to hurt me. We still move in the same circles and I am able to be in the same room with her and chit-chat. I am polite."

"Do you feel compassion for Susan?"

"I understand that she thought she was doing the right thing. I realize she was unhappy then and that affected the situation. I appreciate certain things about her like her intelligence, but I still question her integrity."

"Are you still angry with her?"

"The anger sometimes reappears, but I am aware of it and have it under control. I can empathize more now and I realize that we all mess up."

Jacob admitted that concepts like grace and compassion are difficult for him to embrace. "I tend to expect perfection and focus more on justice than mercy. Humility is difficult as well. The first spontaneous prayer I ever voiced that came straight from my heart was, 'Oh God, help me live with my imperfections.' It's hard for me to live with the fact that I'm not perfect, but I know it's best just to admit it. When I'm working to forgive others I remind myself, 'I've done things I'm not proud of too.'"

Jacob found forgiving himself harder than forgiving others. He told me his greatest impediment to forgiveness was his "perpetual sense of wounded dignity." I asked him how he overcame that.

"I go for a walk, chant, and calm myself so I can see the feeling and separate the feeling from me. I work with the source of the feeling once I've calmed myself. "

"What changes in you when you forgive?" I asked.

"I become quieter. I feel better. I'm able to be in touch with my feelings and emotions and look to a reality beyond. Did you notice the change in my tone when I started talking about forgiving Susan?"

"Yes," I responded without hesitation, for his voice had reflected a clear change in his emotions.

Jacob benefited from the realization that choosing forgiveness was good for him. "If someone cuts me off in traffic, I tell myself I have choices. I can go with my instincts and simply be pissed off, or I can say 'I guess I've done that too.' The guy who cut me off is not hurt by my anger, but I am. So by choosing forgiveness I benefit."

Forgiveness Moves Us Along the Path to Being Who We Are Meant to Be

"Forgiveness makes me more aware of the choices I have and the importance of taking responsibility for those choices. Forgiveness moves me along a path to being who I am."

Jacob shared a story from Zusya, a wise rabbi, that motivated him to forgive.

Before his death, Rabbi Zusya said, "In the world to come,
they will not ask me: 'Why were you not Moses?
Why were you not Abraham?'
They will ask me: 'Why were you not Zusya?'"

Wisdom from the Jewish tradition helped guide Jacob. He explained, "The Torah (first five books of Hebrew scripture) is usually translated as 'The Law,' but it's better translated as 'archery instruction' because it was written to help us find our target—to discover who we are supposed to be. The Hebrew word *chet* is often translated into English as sin, but a *chet* is not an evil act; it's an act that misses its mark and goes astray. Raw anger, meaning anger that I haven't examined, worked with, and transformed into something constructive, intrudes on who I am supposed to be and leads me astray."

Jacob related to me a teaching story from the Cherokee culture that also inspired him to choose forgiveness. "A grandson asks his grandfather how to deal with the fight going on inside him, how to handle the struggle he had with his competing feelings. The grandfather compared those feelings to two wolves battling inside of us, one being mean and angry, the other being kind and generous. The grandson asked which wolf would win, and the grandfather replies, 'The one you feed.' The forgiveness process is like working to feed my good wolf."

In some versions of the Cherokee story the grandfather advises the grandson, "If you feed both wolves well, they both win." Why would we want to feed the evil wolf? Because the side of us that gets angry, sad, jealous, greedy, etc. will not go away. It's part of our neurobiology, a part of who we are. If we try to ignore it or pretend it isn't there, it will just become hungrier, more uncontrollable, and will be sneakily looking for attention and ways to get fed. Both our good and bad wolves need to be attended to and guided. When we take care of both wolves, they can work together instead of fighting, and we can lessen the burden of internal struggle and find peace.

Jacob naturally felt angry because he perceived that he was being blamed and judged unfairly by the ED and by people in the organization's membership. It's especially painful when someone we have trusted hurts us, and the pain is magnified if other people we care about start judging and blaming us as well. The misunderstanding with the ED led to a deep sense of helplessness and anguish, which turned to bitterness and resentment, as he was criticized by others and couldn't defend himself. Jacob knew he needed to let his "bad wolf" work with his "good wolf" and find a solution to the problems he and his organization were dealing with.

Susan's actions were hurtful as were the membership's misconceptions regarding what had happened. Even more concerning can be questioning how our own actions contribute to a painful situation. It's hard to accept our own imperfections. Jacob questioned his own behavior. Should the Board have communicated

BECOMING AWARE OF MY CHOICES: | 223

through Susan's lawyer instead of ending negotiations? What actions may have produced a different result?

Jacob knew that he needed to turn the corner and leave his mistrust and bitterness behind. In his letter to Susan he wrote, "Being human got us here; being human, I trust, will move us into a better place."

Being human is hard, but forgiving each other for our inevitable missteps creates beautiful relationships. At a meeting Jacob attended during Women's History Month, he was asked to describe a woman who was important to him. He chose his wife because, "She tells me it's okay to be who I am, even though she thinks I'm an asshole." He later told his wife what he said and after they both laughed, she amended it to, "It's okay to be who you are, even though I can't relate to everything you are."

We can try to understand others, but sometimes we may not be able to relate to certain aspects of their personalities or situations. Respecting and loving them, honoring who they are and letting them be themselves, is a beautiful gift we can give others. If we are fortunate enough to receive that unconditional love in return, we can feel and express our gratitude.

You Are Not Your Negative Thoughts and Feelings

"What advice would you give someone who had experienced a painful event and was considering whether or not to forgive?" I asked Jacob.

"Resentment is the poison we drink hoping it will kill our enemy," he replied. "Sit with your hurt feelings, become aware of them. Then ask yourself who those feelings are harming. What if you spent your time thinking of something else? Would you be better off?"

"Feelings are feelings—they are not you; they will only be you if you let them. Use your thoughts and feelings to understand and accept what is, so you can be who you are."

After a moment's pause, Jacob added, "But that's easier said than done. Don't expect to be able to fix your hurt easily."

Even if we know bitterness and anger aren't good for us, we may still balk at the idea of actually putting in time and effort to heal ourselves. We have to believe that forgiveness is actually possible so that we will do what we need to do, to be who we are supposed to be.

Jacob chose a definition of forgiveness that he found realistic and doable. "To forgive is to regard offense without rancor," Jacob advised me. "It's about controlling my anger, my rancor, so that I can be who I am supposed to be. So I can work for justice productively, without hurting myself or others."

Jacob placed a high value on justice and doing what's right, which is why he emphasized the importance of *not* using forgiveness to pretend that what's bad is good, or what's wrong is right. That definition of forgiveness will only lead to more hurt and pain, not healing. Genuine forgiveness leads to liberation. "Forgiveness frees me," said Jacob.

Forgiveness can be conceptualized as a disposition, meaning an inherent quality of mind or character. We can all choose to pursue forgiveness in our lives, and with time and effort, forgiveness can become more natural and inherent in our character. "I am calmer than I used to be," reflected Jacob. "I'm not sure if that's because I have a lower testosterone level or because I've grown spiritually."

We both laughed. "Perhaps both," I suggested.

I personally used to hope that I could rid myself of angst and emotional challenges. A new insight or awareness would come to me, as it did Jacob, and I'd think, "Wow, I've finally got life figured out and things will be easier from now on." And many things have gotten easier, but new trials and additional pain and disappointment keep coming my way. I realize I will never have things all figured out, and I don't think that's what life is all about anyway. It's not about a lovely linear progression of delightful events. It's about welcoming change, opening our minds to new perspectives, and creating healthy thoughts and behaviors. There's a lot of power and excitement in that.

Jacob's perspective changed when he became more aware of the effect anger and bitterness had on his life. His journey back to Judaism, the wisdom tradition of his birth, gave him guidance as he worked on forgiving himself and others so that he could be the person he was meant to be. Our next forgiveness hero, Mo Chou, changed her perspective and learned to forgive when she started studying a religion that was new to her, Tibetan Buddhism.

THE POWER OF NEW PERSPECTIVES: MO CHOU'S STORY

When one door of happiness closes, another opens,
but often we look so long in disappointment
and bitterness at the closed door
that we do not expectantly look for, and
therefore see with pleasure and gratitude,
the one which has been opened for us.
—HELEN KELLER

The world religions have all led people to forgiveness, but we may relate better to one religion or sacred belief system than another. We may prefer a certain religion because it's what we grew up with. We have affection for it because it has strengthened and inspired us. There is no reason to change paths if your sacred beliefs are leading you forward with love and compassion.

However, sometimes the religion we were raised with or the beliefs we have been exposed to don't fulfill our needs and we must open a new door. Perhaps we can't identify with the role models or the context of the teachings. Sometimes we've had a bad experience with some of the people in a religion and have been hurt by the way they have interpreted the faith. Many people close the door to organized religion because of its potential to inspire fear and conflict.

Mo Chou, who was 40, grew up Christian in China, but four years before our interview she found her spiritual home in Tibetan Buddhism. I was referred to Mo Chou by one of her Christian friends, and Mo Chou emphasized that her religion inspired her to love all sentient (conscious, feeling) beings, regardless of their beliefs. Mo Chou praised her Buddhist teacher, or khenpo, for helping guide and support her forgiveness journey.

Mo Chou's story begins in China, where she grew up as the only child of a middle class family. She loved her mom very much, but sometimes she hated her dad. "My dad would drink a lot, and after he drank he became angry and mean. He would lose his temper and say hurtful things to my mom and me. Sometimes he would hit my mom."

When Mo Chou graduated from university in China, she decided she wanted to go to the United States. "One of the big reasons was that I wanted to get away from my dad," she told me. Mo Chou passed a test that allowed her to pursue an MBA in America and was excited to be far from her father. The United

States brought big transitions in her life—one being a change in religion.

Buddhism originated in Asia, but Mo Chou started studying Buddhism when she was in the United States. She was living in a rural area so found her khenpo online and learned more about her faith and forgiveness through free online classes. She showed me her statue of Kuan Yin, the Buddhist goddess of compassion and mercy, and gave me a keepsake of the "nice lady," who was very special to her. Kuan Yin means "One who hears the cries of the world."

"What did your khenpo teach you about Buddhism?" I asked.

"My khenpo taught me that Buddhism is mainly concerned with two things. One is compassion. One is wisdom. We are taught to do good things to all sentient beings. That includes our enemies, animals, and the spirit world—any entity that in some way has feelings. If you have compassion, there is no enemy. The world is like one big human being and we want to reduce its suffering. Forgiveness is the one thing that can get rid of the pain in the world."

Belief in Reincarnation and Karma Motivated Forgiveness

Mo Chou's belief in reincarnation and karma motivated her to forgive. According to Buddhism, our souls are reincarnated, meaning reborn, in a new body. Karma is believed to determine our reincarnation, or the nature of our next existence. Karma is a force generated by our thoughts and actions while we are in our earthly bodies. A belief in reincarnation leads those of historically Eastern faiths to conclude that even the worst sins can be forgiven through suffering, experience with life, and multiple reincarnations. Karma implies that problems in life are created because of an individual's own previous behavior. There is no need to seek revenge because justice will come through reincarnation.

"Everything that happens to us is because of karma," Mo Chou said. "I do not blame my dad or anyone else for painful events in my life. It's my own fault."

Mo Chou believed her dad did mean things to her because in another life she had done mean things to him. "Maybe my dad was a pig in his previous life and I ate pork. The pig can feel hatred even if he doesn't speak words. Perhaps my dad wants to be good to me, but he still has hatred in his heart from his past life. As a Buddhist, I need to take responsibility for my own self and not blame others. I need to work on getting rid of any hatred I have."

"How have your beliefs changed the way you interact with your dad?" I asked.

"If my dad says bad things to me, I do not respond. I do not fight back. I have more wisdom and truth now. I know that if I respond to my dad's hurtful words or behaviors with hatred and anger, then in the next life that pattern will continue. The negative pattern will never end unless I work to change it."

"What do you do to change it?" I probed.

"I've been in the United States 15 years and I call my parents at least once a week. It used to be if my dad answered the phone he would just say, 'Your mom's here,' and give her the phone. My dad has no friends and doesn't talk much. Now that I'm practicing compassion, I feel sorry for my dad and realize I should help take care of him. I need to get to know him better. So now I try to talk to him and will ask him about his health and how things are going."

No More Bad Dad

Mo Chou didn't excuse her dad's behavior or pretend what he did was okay. But she did learn to view her father with more compassion, became more appreciative of his positive characteristics, and no longer thought of him as a bad dad. She realized he had sacrificed for his family and done the best he could. "My father learned traditional Chinese values and he is very good to his parents. He has been very generous with money. My father paid for me to go to the United States and I appreciate that."

Mo Chou visits her parents once a year in the summertime with her son. She works hard to make those visits pleasant. "My dad was not pleased that I became Buddhist. Last year he was not feeling happy and was saying mean things. I did not fight back; I kept silent and avoided conflict. I now eat a vegan diet, which my dad doesn't like, so I ordered some good meat dishes for him. I prayed for him and did nice things for him, like wish him good health and give him credit for good things he'd done."

Mo Chou's mother decided to become Buddhist as well and she also prayed for the family and their relationships. A month before our interview, Mo Chou's mother called her with some good news. "Your dad told me that he noticed you had to sit on the cold floor when you were home doing your meditations. He said, 'Let's go shop for a mattress so when Mo Chou comes back home she has a soft place to sit.' I am so happy. Your father has accepted your Buddhism and was so thoughtful."

When people are mean or hurtful to us it's instinctive and easy to simply be mean and hurtful in return. But Mo Chou and her mom believed in karma and were willing to work on changing a negative cycle. Because people often do offensive things when they themselves are hurting or fearful, kind efforts to make them feel accepted and loved may be what they need to let down their defenses and imitate the thoughtful behavior being shown to them.

"How have your feelings for your dad changed?" I asked.

"Before forgiveness I hated and resented my dad and that caused a lot of suffering for me. I would cry a lot. Now that I've become Buddhist, I pray every day and I don't feel the pain I used to feel."

Letting Go of Expectations and Desires

"How have your relationships with other people changed?"

"In the past, when I met new people or talked to friends, I'd be very critical and sensitive. I would interpret people's comments or actions negatively and think things like 'He's mean,' or 'She sounds very nasty.' But step by step, I learned to focus on more positive things about people. Now I feel more free and comfortable with my friends. I can appreciate people's good sides. I have more friends now."

"What about when family or people you know do things that cause you pain or go against your beliefs?" I queried.

"I still forgive them. I think there's no reason to hold that suffering and pain inside. My khenpo has taught me the root of our pain is attachment to certain expectations and ideas. We can choose to let go of the expectations that are causing us pain. For example, in life people may expect to be rich. But you can change your expectations so you are okay with whatever amount of money you have. It's the same with family. If we attach to the idea our husband or children must be a certain way, we will suffer when they don't act according to our desires. If we don't attach to those expectations, we can be free and happy."

When I first started studying and teaching world religions, I struggled with fully understanding and explaining the Buddhist concepts of nonattachment and letting go of expectations and desires. I'd been taught to have high expectations, desire the American dream, set lofty goals and always strive for more. What was the Buddha trying to tell us? Be lazy and don't care about anything?

I discovered that actually, it was just the opposite. The Buddha taught that good mental and spiritual health takes serious and steadfast effort. You can't be lazy and you need to care.

Nonattachment means we don't have temper tantrums when things don't go our way. We adjust to adversity and find a way to deal with the bumps and bruises of life with compassion and forbearance, which together make up the virtue forgiveness. Our words and actions can contribute to a healthy world, or act like a cancer that destroys the body it lives in and therefore ultimately destroys itself.

Letting go of expectations and desires doesn't mean we don't wish for the good things in life. It means accepting life as it is. We are taught rules of behavior and absorb society's goals for us. There are naturally things we hope will happen. But we are not in charge of our world, a world that is constantly changing and that requires us to use our creativity in order to adapt. If we open our minds to healthier perspectives our pain can dissipate and a new door can appear.

Creating New Ways of Thinking and Changing Daily Habits

Mo Chou studied and worked at being compassionate and forgiving. She created new ways of thinking and changed her daily habits. "I read many books and am guided by the words of the wise monks. I feel better because now I eat vegetarian and have lost weight. I meditate, pray, and study each day. If negative thoughts start coming into my mind, I change my focus to the positive. I concentrate on keeping busy with positive things every day so there's no time and no space in my mind for negatives. I listen to gentle music and songs that make me feel compassion."

Mo Chou's Buddhist teachers encouraged her to keep studying because developing healthy mental and spiritual habits takes time and effort. She knew she was developing into a more compassionate person. Her biggest challenge was relaxing expectations of her son and husband so that she would not lose her temper and feel angry with them.

"What do you do when your son or husband doesn't act the way you think he should?" I asked.

"I pray for them, and try to be kind, and realize it's karma and my expectations that are causing my anger. I used to be angry for several days, but now I can usually calm down in about ten minutes. Controlling my temper is hard for me because I am still learning, but I am much better at it."

Mo Chou emphasized the importance of taking control, *not* of other people or events, but of our own minds. "I read and study, which changes my thoughts, and when my thoughts change my feelings change and my actions change. I am learning to control my mind. It's harder to conquer our minds than it is to conquer the world."

Control Your Thoughts So Your Thoughts Don't Control You

Controlling our minds is difficult, and the term mindfulness is now often used to describe how we can do that. Being mindful means being aware of our thoughts so that our thoughts don't control us; we control our thoughts.

It is natural for us to automatically react to stimuli in habitual or instinctive ways that may or may not be healthy. When I am being mindful, I don't judge or try to suppress my thoughts. I also don't assume my thoughts are who I am. Thoughts that come into my head may or may not be beneficial. They may or may not be moral or compassionate. My thoughts are just thoughts, and when I have the courage to confront them I can decide what I want to do with them. My higher self can decide—not my instincts, not my past trauma, not my fears, not my pain, pride, or shame.

When angry, nasty, cowardly type thoughts come into our head, it can be hard to accept them. We worry that our thoughts indicate we are a bad person. But realizing it's natural to have detrimental thoughts leads us to self-compassion. We can become more forgiving, appreciating that we all have trouble being human.

People Focus Too Much on Themselves

I asked Mo Chou how she thought self-forgiveness and forgiveness of others were related. "I try not to pay attention to myself and instead focus on compassion for others," she said. "This world has many problems because people focus too much on themselves. It's important to be patient with others and learn to love them. In Buddhism we believe people can attain higher and higher levels of wisdom and truth and at some point there are no others, we are all one. At the highest level we have wiped our heart clean and are not suffering anymore. We become awakened."

The Buddha spent many years searching for a way to end suffering and become awakened. He was born privileged and wealthy, but switched to asceticism and almost starved himself to death until he came upon the Middle Way. He created a better way of living when he learned that balance was a key to good health.

Mo Chou also found happiness by balancing concern for herself with concern for others. Thinking more of others alleviated much of the suffering Mo Chou had experienced when she was unable to forgive her father and was critical of her friends and family members.

"Buddhism has taught me the wisdom of thinking about others and not worrying so much about myself. If I'm ruining someone else's happiness, it won't benefit me. The best thing I can do for myself is think more of others. We are all connected and are better off when we do good things for each other. Then none of us suffer."

Karma Generates Fairness; Expectations Generate Illusions

Mo Chou summarized for me the two main beliefs that aided her ability to forgive. "One is karma," she said. "My dad has done bad things to me because I did bad things to him in another life, so it's fair. The second is that there is no bad dad. That's just an illusion I created in my mind because of my own expectations for his behavior."

Mo Chou created a new way of thinking, feeling, and behaving that brought her better health, less suffering, more friends, and spiritual growth. She was nurtured by her online Buddhist community and international friends, who helped her become a more patient, compassionate, and forgiving person.

Religious and spiritual connections were vital to Mo Chou's forgiveness journey, but Anna, our next forgiveness hero, was agnostic. The connections that were essential to her came from family.

The Joy of Learning: Anna's Story

Live as if you were to die tomorrow.
Learn as if you were to live forever.
—MAHATMA GANDHI

Learning is one of my favorite things—right up there with eating chocolate and hiking beautiful nature trails. It's exciting to open my mind and heart to new knowledge, new insights, new skills. However, learning can be frightening if I doubt my ability, fear I will be embarrassed, or believe failing makes me a failure. To fully enjoy learning, I have to let go of worries about asking dumb questions, making stupid mistakes, and looking like an idiot to others. I need to banish negative voices in my head, let down my defenses, and allow myself to evolve and mature.

Learning from painful experiences and suffering is very important to our growth and maturity, but it's hard to make that joyful. I really hate it when something hurtful or humiliating happens to me; when life is not going the way I expect it to and confusion and disappointment overwhelm me. I'd rather learn by reading about someone else's suffering and triumph over agony, although I realize that's not as effective as the real thing.

You may be familiar with the quote, "Life is what happens to us when we're making other plans" and the ever popular saying, "Shit happens." When our life story turns to a page we don't like, it's time to have the courage to face and accept whatever happened, try to understand it with a compassionate heart, and reach out to supportive connections. Whether the offensive act can be traced back to ourselves, to others, or to the powers that be, we need to learn some lessons and create a Plan B. Knowing that we have the ability to learn from our pain gives us hope that joy will come eventually. Darkness does not have to last.

Anna's Story

Anna was a 26-year-old engineering student from Norway studying in the United States. She self-identified as agnostic, meaning she claimed neither faith nor disbelief in God. While in the United States, Anna met a young man named Jason, whom she dated for approximately eight months. Their relationship was serious, but in accordance with Anna's college plan, she needed to return to Norway for eight months, which necessitated a physical separation from Jason. Anna and Jason had formed a special bond so they made plans for Jason to cross the ocean and meet her family. Two weeks before his arrival, Jason delivered painful news to Anna. He had cheated on her while she was gone.

Anna was devastated, but also very level headed. She first turned to her mother for guidance. "I had to tell my mom because she would have figured it out one way or another," said Anna. "I talked to my mom a lot about it. It was important to me that if I forgave Jason, she could still accept him as part of the family. My mom said, 'I probably wouldn't forgive him if I were you, but if you forgive him, we are just going to erase that from our memories.' That was definitely vital to me because I am so close to my mom."

Anna was fortunate to have an understanding stepdad. "I'm really close to my stepdad as well as my mom," Anna said. "I didn't tell my biological dad because I was unsure how he would feel about it, but it was nice having another adult to talk to, and a man who cared about me and could give advice. My stepbrother cheated on his fiancé, so my stepdad had gone through discussions with him as well."

Anna said she communicated a lot with her mother and stepdad before she talked to her boyfriend again regarding the issue. They had to decide whether or not Jason should come visit her in Norway.

Anna made her decision and told Jason, "I think the worst thing you could do is *not* come to Norway. The plane tickets are already paid for and we've booked various events that we plan to do. If you don't show up that means you don't think our relationship is going anywhere. There is no way I can forgive you if you don't come."

"Did Jason ask for your forgiveness?" I inquired.

"No," replied Anna. "He said he wasn't looking for forgiveness because he just straight up said, 'I don't think I would forgive you.' That bothered me, but I respected the way he was handling the situation—directly and honestly. He called me a couple days after it happened and told me about it himself over the phone. I had often teased him about being immature, but he was acting very maturely. He had talked to his mom about it, which surprised me. Jason had grown up with only a mom to care for him and they hadn't had an easy relationship. To me, the fact that he'd reached out to his mom for advice told me he really wanted to fix what he did."

Jason came to Norway and Anna explained, "We acted more like friends than anything else because I was so insecure and uncertain as to where we were going at that point. I didn't want to mislead any of us."

Anna and Jason both returned to the same college in the United States. Before the incident, they had signed a lease that located them in the same house, but they each had their own bedroom. It was a difficult situation because Anna was still processing how to handle Jason's infidelity and did not yet feel safe enough to carry on their relationship in the same intimate manner as before the incident. Friends noticed this and asked lots of questions, which made Anna uncomfortable. The questions were also a constant reminder of what had happened.

For Reconciliation to be Advantageous, Trust Needs to be Restored

Anna had to decide not only whether she wanted to forgive, but also whether she wished to reconcile with Jason and resume their romantic relationship. She could decide to forgive, but *not* to reconcile. For reconciliation to truly be advantageous, trust needs to be restored.

"For about six months I worked to see if I could learn to trust Jason again. My mom was so open about the situation. She shared experiences of other couples with me. I was able to look at the situation from multiple viewpoints, but still stay true to myself. Also, my boyfriend didn't push me to figure things out. He was willing to wait for me to make up my mind and was okay kinda being in a relationship and kinda not."

Anna wanted to be sure she had genuinely forgiven Jason. She'd seen other couples break up and get back together, but their relationships seemed insecure and untrusting. Anna didn't want that. "I've seen other people not truly forgiving the person who cheated on them, but staying together. Every time they have a problem with that person, they bring the incident up. They think things like 'He did this one time so maybe he's going to do it again' or 'I'm traveling for a week and he'll be by himself. Is he going to cheat on me again?' I don't want to live like that."

Anna had a close friend that seemed compelled to remind her of the cheating that had caused her pain. "Some people made the situation harder, such as one of our closest friends who to this day, every now and then, brings the incident up. In fact, in the period after it happened, she seemed to talk about it more than we did."

"How did that make the situation harder?" I asked.

"Forgiveness means you are able to move on and let go of the past. Jason and I were working through things and it didn't help to be reminded of past mistakes. Once you've processed a painful event and forgiven, it's important not to keep bringing the offense up in an argument or discussion. Reliving a past hurt or using a past mistake against someone ruins a relationship. If I keep bringing up my past hurt, it means I haven't forgiven."

Anna explained to me that she and Jason both learned a lot and grew closer in the months following the incident. "We had a lot more open dialogue between us. We had more adult-like conversations and matured a lot."

Anna decided that a good test of their relationship would be for her to evaluate her feelings when she went back to Norway for Christmas and Jason stayed in the United States. She thought, "If I go home for Christmas and I'm worried and bothered, I can't do it." Anna felt okay over the holiday break and realized the relationship could work. "So after six months, Jason and I sat down, had a talk, and decided to try again. We moved back in the same room together and kept working on our relationship. We're still together and it's been over a year now."

The phrase "Hell hath no fury like a woman scorned" did not apply to Anna. She was not a proponent of revenge and vindictiveness and tried to be open and listen to Jason's viewpoint. Empathy contributes to our ability to learn and to understand the actions and feelings of others. I asked Anna if she was able to understand Jason's hurtful behavior.

"I felt like I did. I realized we hadn't known each other for a long period of time before I had to leave, and then we had to live on two different continents for an equally long period of time.

I understand that a person misses being close to someone in a relationship, just being able to hold someone's hand. I think I was especially devastated because he cheated on me two weeks before we would be together again and I was so looking forward to his visit. But I tried to look at the whole picture and not just the painful incident."

Anna felt deep hurt when she found out Jason had cheated on her, but she knew she didn't want to cause hurt in return. "If I was going the revenge route I wouldn't have respected me. I would have had regrets if I had acted bitterly. There are two players in a game and if one of them plays badly and then the other one plays badly, it's just a bad game overall and it's not going to go anywhere."

"I felt so much pain," said Anna. "I couldn't imagine hurting Jason that much. But I did want him to know how much I was hurting. That's why the long waiting period was so important. He needed to know what he did was not at all right and that I couldn't just jump back into our relationship."

"How do you feel about the incident right now?" I asked.

"Now I don't even think about it unless it gets brought up. And when I do think about it, I don't feel mad and I don't get sad. Jason and I learned a lot from each other. The whole process of forgiving and accepting what happened has helped us grow. I now think it's okay this happened because we got some good things out of it in the end." Anna smiled. "Maybe that's the engineering part of me, focused on the end product."

Don't Worry; Problem Solve

"What are some of the important things you learned?" I asked.

"It definitely taught me that if you take your time, you can find a way forward. My family is really talkative, but I'm more reflective so I like to think through things. I listen to people's perspectives, but then I step back and see how I feel when I am by myself. I let my thoughts wander and see what comes into my head. For the first couple of months after I found out Jason cheated on me the incident came into my head all the time, but gradually things got better. I knew I'd processed things sufficiently when I had a six-hour drive by myself and didn't think about the incident a single time. I was ready to move on."

Moving from the decision to forgive a major transgression to deeply and emotionally forgiving takes time. But could it take too much time?

"Yes," said Anna. "Setting a time limit was important to my mental health. I've learned to take my time, but also give myself time limits. For example, if I haven't figured my problem out in a month, I need to take action or shake things up. Maybe a new conversation needs to happen or I need to create a different way of thinking about something. I problem solve instead of just worrying about something."

Listen to Your Inner Voice and Be True To It

Anna was agnostic, but she agreed with religious and spiritual sages that wisdom and insights often come when we are quiet, still, and receptive to the voices and feelings inside of us. Persons who are religious or spiritual may call that 'listening for the voice of God or a higher power.' Anna thought of it as listening to her inner truth and stressed the importance of being true to herself.

What gets in the way of reflection and taking the time to listen to our inner voice? Anna thought that technology was one impediment. "It seems like technology pops up everywhere, demanding our attention and greedy for our time. I have my phone with me all the time. However, when I was going through my forgiveness experience I often forgot about my phone because I had so many thoughts in my head that needed processing."

Obsessive negative thoughts can also crowd out rational, balanced thoughts. It's instinctive to focus on what we don't like about people who've hurt us. But the forgiveness heroes I interviewed learned to appreciate the positive things about their offenders. They didn't put people in boxes labeled "good person" or "bad person" and use duct tape to ensure they couldn't escape. Instead, they strived to find the aspects of their offender they appreciated. This is especially important when dealing with family or friends with whom we want or need to continue a relationship.

"I can thank my boyfriend for helping me become a better person," said Anna. "Jason is so straightforward and honest. I know that if something is wrong, he is going to tell me about it. I've definitely learned a lot from him about being genuine and open."

Creating New Ways of Thinking and Stronger Relationships
Anna was able to take a very painful incident and turn it into a very important learning experience. Her experience left her

stronger and more confident in her problem-solving ability. "I think in a different way than I did before. I'd never had a problem before in which I consulted other people the way I did in this case. Now I can reach out to people in my life without being scared or worried about what they will tell me. I don't want to feel like a victim and just have people say, 'Oh, I feel so sad for you' and pity me. And I don't want people to just tell me what to do."

"What I need is people who will listen without judging and who will give me different perspectives," said Anna. "When something painful happens, it's easy to get caught up in the moment and have some irrational thoughts. Supportive people help me calm down and make better decisions."

Going through a painful experience with a supportive person provides an opportunity to grow closer to that person. Anna valued the strong bond she had with her mother and was able to grow closer to her stepfather. "I got way closer to my stepdad because he was such a good person to talk to regarding the whole situation. He'd been my stepdad for 17 years, but I felt we were able to bond in a different way that was good for both of us. We sat down together and he was able to give me advice, which I listened to as much as I did the advice my mom gave me. It made him feel good that he was able to help me. When I go home, it's noticeable that we're closer to each other. I don't usually use the word spiritual," Anna said, laughing, "but I'm going to anyway. We became closer in a spiritual way."

Going through a tough situation together creates strong bonds between people. We feel gratitude for those people who share life's bumps and bruises with us and we learn the value of trust. Our feelings for those who love and support us through challenging times are hard to describe in words, but are deeply felt in terms of a spiritual or soul connection.

Anna didn't subscribe to a certain religion, but she certainly had sacred beliefs and values. I asked her what role her cultural values and belief system played in her forgiveness experience. "I've grown up with so many religions," she responded. "My mom is agnostic, my dad is Christian, my grandma is Catholic, my grandfather on my mom's side is Muslim. So I've learned from different religions and I like to practice meditation now and then. My mom and I believe there's some kind of higher power we can't describe; that's why we're agnostic instead of atheists. I think at the end of the day, the important thing is that you stay true to yourself."

Staying True to Oneself and Resisting Pressure

But it's not always easy to stay true to oneself and discern the best way to handle a situation and move forward. "It's hard for me to forgive," said Anna, "if I can't have an open conversation with the other person and be genuine and sincere. It's also hard if people pressure me to forgive because I don't want to disappoint people. I don't like feeling torn between staying true to myself and doing what others expect of me."

People may pressure us to forgive because they are uncomfortable with discord or negative emotions. They hope the difficult situation will simply go away and be forgotten, not realizing the danger of repressing hurt and pain. Others may pressure us to forgive because our distress is inconvenient for them. They may fear that dealing with an issue will upset a status quo that is beneficial to them, even if it is not for us.

"How do you handle the pressure?" I asked Anna.

"I've gotten better at accepting the fact that people may expect me to act one way or another. But I realize that I don't have to take their views personally. I remind myself that I'm the one who has to live with myself and the thoughts and feelings that will result from my decisions. But still, I don't like hurting people and sometimes that happens."

If we want to make others happy, we might go along and try to convince ourselves as well as others that an offense is no big deal or doesn't really hurt. But if we bury our pain, we may just end up with more forgiveness work to do because now we're mad at the people who stressed us as well as the original offenders.

"Sometimes it's hard not to resent the people pressuring you," said Anna. "But I'm better now at making my own decisions and moving forward. In the past, I often didn't stay true to myself and went along with others instead of being guided by my inner voice. I had regrets and wasn't as forgiving because I was doing and saying things just to please others, so I was feeling resentful. Now I accept the fact that I did something or that I chose one direction instead of the other and I go with it."

Like Lisa and Esther, Anna became more forgiving when she learned to stand up for herself and confront difficult issues with courage. She had tried to avoid conflict with others, but ended up increasing the conflict in her own mind. Now that she's stronger and more confident, people are less able to hurt her and she doesn't feel like a victim. If we aren't hurt, there is nothing we need to forgive.

Mistakes Are Learning Experiences

Forgiveness is all about learning how to accept mistakes and recover from poor choices. Anna was fortunate to have a family that laid a firm foundation in that regard. "I've always gotten my parents' support regardless of what my choices have been. Even if they have been really bad choices, they've always let me make my own mistakes. They would give me advice and warn me not to do certain things, but they didn't stop me from doing them. And when things didn't work out, they were always there for me. They didn't say things like, 'Well, we told you so.' It was more like, 'Okay, this happened. We know how much it hurts and we are going to be here for you.' So I'm definitely not afraid to make mistakes or to learn because I know I always have that support system around me regardless of what I do."

At times, Anna still found herself ruminating over past regrets. I asked her how she dealt with that. "I tell myself it's not going to do any good to think about the past when I can be focused on improving the future instead. It's over and done. And then," she said, laughing, "I go for a run." Physical exercise helps our bodies produce neurotransmitters that contribute to positive, productive thoughts.

Anna said forgiving others is harder for her than self-forgiveness. "I definitely spend more time thinking about forgiving others," Anna said. "It's hard to know how to improve a relationship or handle a conflict. It takes more processing time for me to understand others than to understand myself. I try to figure out the other person's perspective and work to make it a good learning experience for both of us."

"How do you define forgiveness?" I asked.

"Accepting whatever happened that hurt you, learning from it, and figuring out a way to keep moving forward so you're not dwelling in the past. When I forgive I feel lighter and can focus on more positive, important things. If I keep thinking about whatever the painful event was, I haven't yet figured out how to solve my problem and forgive."

How Do I Keep Forgiving When It's Such Hard Work?

Shield of defensiveness and pride—we use it to attack.
Shield of shame and denial—we use it to hide behind.
Shield of love and compassion—we use it
to keep pain and disappointment
from piercing and shrinking our hearts.

As I was writing this book, I continued to have new experiences that required me to practice forgiveness, some of which demanded hard work and really stretched my abilities. Why did I continue to choose forgiveness? Because I didn't like my other options. Giving up and burying my head in shame seemed cowardly. Blaming, seeking revenge, having a temper tantrum, or playing victim wouldn't improve my situation or state of mind. So I plunged onward, connecting to sources that provided me with guidance and support and that reminded me to be grateful for my blessings. Summoning up my courage even though I was scared. Practicing compassion and stilling the bitter voices that rose up inside me. Keeping my mind open to new ideas and insights that allowed me to learn, grow, and create a better way forward.

I choose forgiveness because the only thing I feel really certain of is that love is the ultimate law of life. That saying adorns my refrigerator along with magnets designed to inspire or make me smile. Magnet sayings include:

> *Some people walk in the rain, others just get wet.*
> *Put your big girl panties on and deal with it.*
> *Kindness is the honey of life.*
> *I have never known any distress that an*
> *hour's reading did not relieve.*

The last quote was written by Charles De Montesquieu before Facebook and Twitter existed. An hour's reading on social media may create more, not less, distress, but well-chosen literature has a calming, healing effect on me. If I need a smile and a good laugh, humorous animal videos are an excellent option.

I know that my ability to forgive depends on fueling up with positive experiences and gratitude; converting anger energy into forgiveness energy; remembering what I value and what brings warmth to my soul. I need help in order to tackle my demons and I can't be afraid to ask for assistance.

It's okay that we don't always feel okay. Processing forgiveness takes time and involves struggle. My inner demons are not going to move out of the neighborhood, so I need to learn how to get along with them and convert them into friends.

Supporting Others in Their Forgiveness Journey

When I'm with others who are struggling with forgiveness, it's important that I stay present and supportive, not dictatorial or controlling. Genuine forgiveness is very personal and can't be rushed.

One day, after giving a presentation on forgiveness, a man came up to me and said he enjoyed my presentation. I wondered which "words of wisdom" were especially important to him. His answer was a little surprising to me. "It was great to hear you say true forgiveness is not easy and takes time. I'm a recovering alcoholic. Forgiveness of both myself and others is a real struggle. It's even harder when people are impatient with me and think I should just be able to get over things. When they do that I can't help but feel additional shame and anger because I can't just let go. Forgiveness is hard and it helps when people understand that. It helps to be supported and to know what I'm feeling is okay. That gives me hope."

Sometimes we want so much for people to feel and behave better that we unwittingly make things worse by pressuring them. It's hard to be patient and it's hard to accept that much of our learning has to be done through experience, and experience requires time. As a parent, I've often wanted to save my children from life's painful lessons, but at times I have made things worse instead of better by going long on words and short on silence.

One of my biggest parenting challenges has been keeping my mouth shut and just being present.

People everywhere need help forgiving, and I recently read an inspiring article about how Zimbabwe was dealing with its need for mental health helpers. They lacked funding to hire as many professionals as would be ideal so decided to recruit and train grandmothers to conduct therapy sessions outside on wooden seats known as Friendship Benches.[28] They chose grandmothers because they are good at listening and guiding people toward solutions, instead of just telling people what to do. The grandmothers facilitated a search for inner truth and peace of mind.

The Easter Story: Resurrection and Redemption

Inspirational stories can help us forgive. The death and resurrection story of Jesus has provided many Christians with assurance that no matter what sins they have committed in the past or will commit in the future, they will be forgiven. In brief, the Easter story relates that God sent his only son, Jesus, to earth because he loved his human creation dearly, but was often very mad at them because they were constantly sinning. During the first century, when Jesus was on earth, it was common for lambs to be sacrificed in atonement for sins. Jesus, the son of God, became the lamb of God who was sacrificed for the sins of humankind with the goal of bringing us humans a new relationship with God the Father. Jesus was crucified by Roman oppressors and died a human death, but arose from the grave, showing his disciples he had been resurrected.

I personally receive comfort and inspiration from the Easter story when I don't try to analyze it scientifically or take it too literally. During the days when the books of the Bible were written, it was common for people to explain difficult concepts through stories, as there was no science as we know it now. Human beings have always sought understanding, meaning, and explanations, but they have not always had universities full of books and laboratories or access to facts that could be scientifically verified. They often used symbolism, metaphors, and teaching stories (parables) to make sense of the world.

I imagine myself back in the days of Jesus. Back then, just as now, it was hard to be human. People struggled with the same questions. How do we deal with guilt and shame? How can we keep going, knowing we have done wrong? Who could love us, wretches that we are? Who can save us from ourselves? We have always desperately needed hopeful, love-inspired answers to those questions, and the Easter story has provided many people with reassuring, encouraging answers over the centuries.

Jesus's resurrection represents being forgiven and born again. It is okay that we are human and do things we regret. It's all good. We can start anew. "Today is the first day of the rest of your life" is a popular saying because we need reassurance that all is not lost when our shame and despair is trying to convince us to give up. We can summon up our courage and keep trying if we know there's a loving spirit, a divine presence, guiding and supporting us.

I personally don't have a lot of faith in sacrificial lambs and placating angry father gods, but I don't think that's what the Easter story is really about. I think it's a story that was meant to illustrate the power of love and compassion, the happiness that comes with forgiving and being forgiven, and the transformation that is possible when we have the courage to create a new and better tomorrow.

The beauty of stories is that we can interpret them in different ways based on what we have experienced and where we are at developmentally. We can learn by listening to how different people understand the same story. For example, in my younger years I didn't like seeing the bloody images of Jesus on the cross with thorns on his head. I couldn't figure out why people would like to see a disturbing image of suffering and pain. I liked the painting I'd grown up with in my church of a well-groomed Jesus in a beautiful field with cute little children and fluffy white lambs surrounding him.

Then I talked to people whose lives had been filled with bloodshed and thorns of some kind and became enlightened. The image of Jesus suffering on the cross was beautiful to them, not because they liked to see anyone suffer, but because it represented the empathy of a divine being who was willing to sacrifice himself for them. Jesus had been willing to feel their pain. He had been betrayed, unfairly judged, and crucified. He was part of a beleaguered population that was being oppressed by a powerful empire. He suffered and knew anguish and he genuinely realized how hard it is to be human. While enduring the excruciating pain of crucifixion, Jesus was still able to ask that his crucifiers be forgiven because, as he said from the cross, "They know not what they do."

The people I talked to were comforted and reassured by the Easter story because it illustrated to them that God gets it. God realizes life on earth is hard and we need lots of love and support from the Divine along the way so we can become better people.

I have listened to people who have been transformed by the Easter story because the meaning it held for them was that Jesus, God, really loved them. It's a wonderful thing to feel loved and some of the people I talked to had never felt anyone cared about them. It was good news that Jesus was willing to die a painful, humiliating death on the cross because he loved them so much. It was life changing to learn Jesus didn't care about what they'd done—whether it was good or bad. He didn't care what other people thought of them or what shameful thoughts or deeds they may be hiding about themselves. The love that transformed them had to do with compassion, mercy, and hope for a new and better tomorrow. It freed them from worries about judgment and abandonment and allowed them to forgive themselves and whoever and whatever else needed forgiving.

Do Your Beliefs Lead You to Love and Kindness?

When my daughters asked questions about whether certain religious beliefs were true or false, I asked them if believing what was being suggested would lead them to be more loving and kind. If they were being led to love, the belief was probably fulfilling a good purpose, whether or not it could be proven scientifically true or accurate. If they were being led to judge others or themselves harshly, exclude instead of include, become fearful or hateful, then they should question the belief.

All the major religions encourage us to forgive, but that doesn't mean we actually do it. The Easter story may or may not lead to genuine forgiveness, depending on how we interpret it and what emotions it inspires in us. It can lead us to forgiveness if we decide to take up our own cross and follow the challenging but hopeful example Jesus set of loving, forgiving, and conquering our fears. It can inspire us if it helps us feel loved and forgiven so that we in turn want to love and forgive others. It can transform us if it helps us believe new beginnings are possible both for ourselves and those we are having trouble forgiving.

We keep forgiving by continually connecting to whatever and whoever leads us from a bleak midwinter to a bright new spring and regrowth. Open minds and open hearts help us move forward with courage and compassion, creating heroic forgiveness tales. Belief in the power of forgiveness motivates us to do the head work and the heart work needed to improve our health and relationships and maintain our integrity.

CREATING NEW THOUGHTS AND BEHAVIORS: HEAD WORK

True forgiveness is when you can say,
"Thank you for that experience."
—OPRAH WINFREY

We are born with certain inborn reflexes and instincts, abilities, and potentials. But most importantly, we are born ready to grow and learn; to adapt to changing circumstances and to evolve into maturity. We are works in progress until the day we die—and possibly after that as well. It's never too late to forgive and be forgiven. Keep becoming. The journey is the destination.

Controlling our minds is a skill emphasized by all the major religions and wisdom traditions. Self-control is a fruit of the spirit. However, being the CEOs (chief executive officers) of our minds may be more difficult than being the CEO of a Fortune 500 company. We have to calm our fears, confront a past that may contain trauma and regrets, maneuver our way through a myriad of different viewpoints and outside pressures, deal with our weaknesses, decide between numerous options—all while keeping our bodies healthy and strong. To sum it all up, being human is hard.

Forgiveness is about head work: thoughts, behaviors, and emotions affect each other in a reciprocal pattern. What I think determines how I feel, and how I feel affects what I think. How I think and feel determines what I do. What I do determines experiences I will have that in turn affect how I think and feel.

For example, if I negatively ruminate about how awful my spouse is, I will probably treat him unkindly, which will likely lead to bad behavior on his part. That bad behavior will make me feel worse and further my negative thoughts and feelings toward him. A vicious cycle may develop.

But I can try to create a positive cycle by doing something nice for my spouse even though I'm mad at him. This is where the saying "Fake it 'til you make it" comes in. My spouse hopefully responds favorably to my acts of kindness, making me feel better, and creating loving thoughts in my mind. Our relationship improves.

It's easy to be critical and unforgiving of others when they are doing things we believe are wrong or that hurt us. Our first reaction is often to tell them just how messed up they are and shun them in some way.

Joking Cousins

In the 13th century, it is said that a king in the Mali Empire of West Africa realized the importance of conquering instinctive impulses and reducing tensions between the different ethnic groups in his domain. The king was aware of our human tendency to judge harshly those who look or do things differently than we do, who compete with us for resources, or who offend us in some way. He knew arrogance and egotism fueled conflict and unrest, while humility and forgiveness nourished peace and prosperity. Therefore he encouraged his people to become joking cousins or *sinankus*.

Sinankus have helped Malians work together peacefully over the centuries. If you travel to Mali today, you will often hear laughter and feel the camaraderie between the various people who live there as they make fun of each other based on their names and the heritage that name represents. You may be accused of eating too many beans, which creates merriment based on the fact that passing gas seems to be a universally funny phenomenon. Your name may indicate you are fat, stupid, a peanut farmer, a slave, etc. People on a hot, dirty, crowded bus may start a joking cousins' conversation, which reduces frowns and grumbles and leads to smiles and laughter.[29]

The people in Mali have found a way to recognize the human desire to feel superior and be judgmental and defuse it through silly jokes. Joking cousins don't take themselves too seriously and they release normal tension through laughter. They bond together through jokes, in the same way close friends and family members show affection through good-natured kidding. What a wonderful feeling when we let down our defenses and view our baser instincts with humor.

Gratitude Fuels Forgiveness

Humility and humor help us forgive and so does gratitude. When I first started researching forgiveness, I viewed gratitude as something peripheral to the process. But the more I researched, interviewed, and examined my own experience, the greater I appreciated the role of gratitude.

Gratitude helps me through the times when I've been shamed or deeply hurt by others. I work at thankfulness and appreciating the moment instead of lamenting my past and worrying about my future. I remember an aha moment when my tolerance for unhappiness was at a low point. My life resembled a train wreck at the time, but I realized I could still enjoy my books, bike rides, and the beauty of the earth. I could play the piano and sing at the top of my voice and after that eat ice cream. I could be kind and treasure precious moments. When I practice gratitude, my hurt and pain dissipates for a while and my mind and spirit open up to new insights—to forgiveness.

Gratitude allows me to put my pain in perspective. I know my life could be oh so much worse as well as better. Realizing the violence, disease, trauma, and discord many others have faced and are facing helps me adjust my attitude and count my blessings. Throughout time and place, the human race has had a tough time of it. Connections, courage, compassion, and creativity help us through those tough spots.

Regrets Are the Realization of What We Need to Learn from the Past So We Can Improve the Future

Has anyone ever told you, "You should have known better"? Have you ever told yourself that? I have and it can lead to misery and self-recrimination. Instead, remind yourself that we all do the best we can with what we know and with whom we are at any given time. We can strive to say, "I know better *now* because I've learned from my painful experience."

Regrets are just the realization of what we need to learn from the past so we can improve the future. Bad decisions can turn into great learning opportunities. And seemingly good decisions may turn out to have harmful consequences. Forgiveness helps us accept the uncertainties in our wild, crazy world.

Endurance, Stamina, Forbearance

A relative sent a Christmas greeting to me last year, noting she and her husband would be celebrating their 93rd birthdays in the next two months. What struck me was the closing wish: "We pray you are feeling well and enduring life." Feeling well (not awesome) and *enduring* life? Is that it? Don't they want me to have peace, prosperity, joyfulness, happiness, success, and the best year ever? Shouldn't they be sharing high expectations for an amazing life and all my wishes coming true?

Maybe not. After all, the Buddha said our desires and expectations are the cause of suffering.

What if, instead of the popular "Have a good day" standard departure line, we said "Endure the day"? I've never been very comfortable with "Have a good day" even though I do use it to end a conversation. I know the sentiment behind it is sincere, but it still seems a little demanding to me. It's not always easy to have a good day and I don't need the pressure. The saying seems a little condescending as well. Does someone think I'm going to try to have a bad day and need to be set straight?

I'm obviously overthinking this and being a bit silly, but I might actually prefer the endure wish if I'm going through a tough time. Sometimes enduring life is as good as it gets, especially when the aches and pains and inevitable disappointments of life challenge us. Endurance signifies strength and forbearance, and there are no worries about my day not being happy or good enough.

What does all that have to do with forgiveness? Buddhists sometimes use compassion and forbearance as partner synonyms for forgiveness. If we expect life to be all happiness and success, we may be unable to accept that being human is hard. We may reach for a pill, strike out in anger, isolate ourselves, or choose some other unproductive activity to escape from sorrow and disappointment. But if we endure and do the headwork necessary to forbear through the tough times, while hanging on to love, compassion, and gratitude to fuel that endurance, we can spark joy and have a good day. And we can be proud of ourselves for choosing forgiveness.

FAITH, HOPE, AND LOVE: HEART WORK

For where your treasure is, there your heart will be also.
—LUKE 12:34

What do you treasure? What words do you hope describe you? Who are you? Being forgiving is tied to our identity, to who we are. I'm not talking about whether you want to be a famous performer, detail-oriented accountant, renowned scientist, or powerful politician. I'm talking about what virtues you hope describe you. What's in your heart? What are your values?

Forgiveness is not a desire or much of a concern for some people. I've spoken with people who are very proud of not forgiving and believe the world is made up of good and bad people. No way are they going to forgive bad people. Some like being feisty and telling people off; they want to be very sure no one ever takes advantage of them. Others like drama and get a high from conflict. Sometimes people are rewarded for being victims and are positively reinforced for *not* forgiving. And I've had some people tell me they simply have had fairly easy lives that haven't required much forgiveness.

We're all on our own journey and at different places in our lives, experiencing different environments with our many diverse personalities. We choose whether or not we want to be forgiving of ourselves, of others, of whatever power may have created our sometimes crazy, sometimes beautiful world. Head work helps us decide what to choose and what actions to take, but ultimately forgiveness is about the heart. What gives us peace of mind? What soothes our soul? What brings us light from darkness?

Life continually challenges us. Change is a constant. Our environment will not stay the same and we will need to adapt. But as the Bible verse (1 Corinthians 13:13) goes, these three will remain: faith, hope, and love. And the greatest of these is love.

Marianne Williamson is quoted as saying, "Until we have seen someone's darkness, we don't really know who they are. Until we have forgiven someone's darkness, we don't really know what love is." It's much easier to be kind and caring when things are going our way and people are acting the way we think they should act. But how comforting and joyful it is to receive love even when we know we've been behaving badly. How brave and beautiful it is to extend forgiveness when we've been treated badly.

Our connections to the sacred and to supportive people provide us with a foundation for faith. We need faith so we can courageously confront and conquer the demons in our life; whether they are coming from inside or outside of us. Faith in ourselves, faith in our beliefs, faith in the power of forgiveness moves us forward because we are taking responsibility for who we are and what we do.

Forgiveness is about our hope that we can and will create inspiring new chapters in our life story. It's hope that we can learn from our mistakes and our suffering. Hope that we and others can grow and evolve; that pain won't last and can be transformed into something precious. Hope that love can triumph over hate.

Among faith, hope, and love, the greatest of these is love because there is no forgiveness without the compassion, kindness, and grace love bestows upon us. Love creates the energy that fuels forgiveness and is also an energy created from forgiveness. Love not only is the greatest attribute, it feels the greatest because we've dropped our defenses, accepted our humanness, and decided to share kindness and light with those around us. If love and forgiveness don't feel great to you, perhaps you just need more time for your heart to figure them out.

Recently I was feeling grouchy and was definitely not in a forgiving mood. I decided to drink some tea. I have the tea bags with tags that provide a little wisdom along with the brew. My tea bag said, "Your greatest happiness is based on the warmth of your heart." I thought about that and realized the tea bag was right. I could make myself feel better by focusing on love. I decided to do something nice for a friend who I knew needed some extra attention and I prayed for a person who saddened and discouraged me because I knew they needed extra attention as well. In other words, I worked on warming up my heart, which in turn turned on my happiness switch. I felt forgiving.

Love Means Never Having to Say You're Sorry

You may have heard the phrase, "Love means never having to say you're sorry," which originated with the 1970 movie *Love Story*. The saying never made much sense to me, but I didn't give it too much thought either. Thinking about it now, I'd say the statement makes sense if I emphasize the word *having* and read it as, "Love means never *having* to say you're sorry."

I like saying "I'm sorry." It lessens my guilt and that makes me feel better. I don't like hurting people. It makes me feel ashamed. If I can acknowledge my bad behavior and make amends, I am happier. If I make a genuine apology, the person I offer it to can feel safer—assuming I've learned from the experience and will be better behaved in the future. Trust can be restored and the relationship can grow and improve.

But sometimes I may be rather clueless and erroneously regard my bad behavior as good. Words I thought were kind come off as condescending. I don't offer help when I should because I am absorbed with my own issues. Pride or ignorance may be blocking my ability to empathize or understand a different perspective. If that is the case, I hope my family and friends will love me and forgive my oblivious state of mind.

We may wish some people would say "I'm sorry" more often, but we can still love them dearly. Sometimes we perceive something as hurtful, but the other person thinks they're just stating facts. Sometimes someone takes what we say as criticism, but we believe we're just expressing an opinion. Boundless forgiveness may be necessary as we create new chapters in the book we are writing together with those we love.

When we love people unconditionally, they don't *have* to say they're sorry. We understand people don't necessarily mean what they say when they're angry or stressed or uninformed. We realize people get cranky, go through trauma and tough times, and really mess up. Fragile egos and being clueless sometimes prevent a genuine apology. But love is at its most miraculous when saying "I'm sorry" isn't mandatory.

When the Head Is Being Too Judgmental, the Heart Needs to Take Charge

Our head may tell us what we or someone else did is wrong, is horrible, is unforgiveable. And our head may very well be accurate about that behavioral evaluation. Our head may attach the bad behavior to the person associated with it and they in turn become horrible and unforgivable people. If our head is judging us personally the guilt can be unbearable.

That's when our heart needs to come to the rescue, take charge, and choose forgiveness. When we connect with a kind and loving heart, grace triumphs over shame. Acceptance over rejection. Empathy over apathy. Love over hate. Light over darkness.

When we connect with the light and make peace with our demons, we gain the courage to break free of shame and fix problems, not blame. Compassion guides our thinking, not bitterness and anger. We are able to create a new and better way forward that will improve our personal well-being, better our relationships, and transform our lives. Connections, courage, compassion, and creativity empower us and make genuine forgiveness possible.

WE ARE NO LONGER VICTIMS;
WE ARE FORGIVENESS HEROES.

ABOUT THE AUTHOR

Christy Heacock, PhD, is a research psychologist and educator who has personally experienced the transformative power of forgiveness. Her work weaves together wisdom from the world's religions and wisdom traditions with neuroscience and cognitive psychology. Chris has been married 37 years to her husband Roger and has two adult daughters and a stepson. Joys include bicycling, hiking, singing, playing the piano, traveling, and lifelong learning.

Chris is available for presentations and workshops. You may contact her through her website, chooseforgiveness.com.

NOTES

1   Freke, T. (1998). *The illustrated book of sacred scriptures.* Wheaton, IL: Theosophical Publishing House.

2   Adamos, M. M., & Griffin, J. B. (2013). What do we mean by 'forgiveness?': Some answers from the ancient Greeks. In McKenry, T., & Thingholm, C.B.(Eds.). *Forgiveness: Philosophy, psychology, and the arts.* Retrieved from http://philpapers.org/archive/ADAWDW.pdf

3   Jenkins, P. (2017, June 26). Twelve questions: Patty Jenkins, *Time*, 56.

4   VonDrehle, D. Newton-Small, J. & Rhodan, M. (November 23, 2015). Murder, race and mercy: Stories from Charleston, *Time*, 42-68.

5   Thompson, M.J. (2014). *Forgiveness: A Lenten study.* Louisville, KY: Westminster. John Knox Press, p. 51.

6   VonDrehle, D. Newton-Small, J. & Rhodan, M. (November 23, 2015). Murder, race and mercy: Stories from Charleston, *Time*, 42-68.

7   VanderWeele, T.J. (2018). Is forgiveness a public health issue? *American Journal of Public Health*, 108(2), pp. 189-190. doi: abs/10.2105/AJPH.2017.304210

8   Scull, N.C. (2015). Forgiveness, revenge, and adherence to Islam as moderators for psychological well-being and depression among survivors of the 1990 Iraqi invasion of Kuwait. *Journal of Muslim Mental Health*, 9(1), 2015. doi:10.3998/jmmh.10381607.0009.103

9   Sapmaz, F.,Yıldırım, M., Topçuoğlu, P., Nalbant, D. & Sızır, U. (2015, December 20). Gratitude, forgiveness and humility as predictors of subjective well-being among university students, *International Online Journal of Educational Sciences*. Retrieved from http://www.iojes.net/userfiles/Article/IOJES_1764.pdf

10 Korner, A., Coroiu, A., Copeland, L., Gomez-Garibello, C., Albiani, C., Zenger, M. Brahler, E. (2015). The role of self-compassion in buffering symptoms of depression in the general population, *Plos One*. Retrieved from http://journals.plos.org/plosone/article?id=10.1371/journal.pone.0136598

11 Bies, R. J., Barclay, L. J., Saldanha, M. F., Kay, A.A., & Tripp, T. M. (2018). Trust and distrust: Their interplay with forgiveness in organizations. In R.H. Searle, A. I. Nienaber, & S. B Sitkin, (Eds.), *The Routledge Companion to Trust* (pp. 302-326). New York, NY:Routledge.

12 Watts F, Dutton K, Gulliford L. (2006). Human spiritual qualities: Integrating psychology and religion. *Mental Health, Religion & Culture*, 9(3), pp. 277-289. doi: 10.1080/13694670600615524

13 Dweck, C. S., & Leggett, E. L. (1988). A social-cognitive approach to motivation and Personality. *Psychological Review*, 95(2), 256-73.

14 Rusk, N., Tamir, M., & Rothbaum, F. (2011). Performance and learning goals for emotion regulation. *Motivation and Emotion*, 35(4), 444-460. doi: 10.1007/s11031-011-9229-6

15 Dweck, C. S., & Leggett, E. L. (1988). A social-cognitive approach to motivation and Personality. *Psychological Review*, 95(2), 256-73.

16 Anderman, E. (2015). Goal orientation theory. *Education.com*. Retrieved from http://www.education.com/reference/article/goal-orientation-theory/

17 Ellis, A. (1998). *Three methods of rational emotive behavior therapy that make my psychotherapy effective*. Retrieved from http://files.eric.ed.gov/fulltext/ED424516.pdf

18 Gobodo-Madikizela P. (2018) Forgiveness is 'the wrong word': Empathic repair and the potential for human connection in the aftermath of historical trauma. In M. Leiner & C. Schliesser (Eds.), *Alternative approaches in conflict resolution: Rethinking peace and conflict studies* (pp. 111-123). Palgrave Macmillan: UK. doi: 10.1007/978-3-319-58359-4_11

19 Lavelock, C. R., Worthington Jr., E. L., Davis, D. E., Griffin, B. J., Reid, C. A., Hook, J. N., & Van Tongeren, D. R. (2014). The quiet virtue speaks: An intervention to promote humility. *Journal of Psychology and Theology, 42(1)*, 99-110.

20 Umbreit, M. S., Blevins, J., Lewis, T. (2015). *The energy of forgiveness: Lessons from those in restorative dialogue.* Eugene, OR: Cascade Publications.

21 Lavelock, C. R., Worthington Jr., E. L., Davis, D. E., Griffin, B. J., Reid, C. A., Hook, J. N., & Van Tongeren, D. R. (2014). The quiet virtue speaks: An intervention to promote humility. *Journal of Psychology and Theology, 42(1)*, 99-110.

22 Emmons, R. A. (2000). Is spirituality an intelligence? Motivation, cognition, and the psychology of ultimate concern. *International Journal for the Psychology of Religion,* 10(1), 3-26. doi:10.1207/S15327582IJPR1001_2

23 Thompson, L. Y., Snyder, C. R., Hoffman, L., Michael, S.
    T., Rasmussen, H. N., Billings, L. S., Heinze, L., Neufeld,
    J. E., Shorey, H. S., Roberts, J. C., Roberts, D. E. (2005).
    Dispositional forgiveness of self, others, and situation.
    Journal of Personality 73(2), 313-359. doi: 10.1111/j.1467-
    6494.2005.00311.x

24 Riek, B. M., & Mania. E. W. (2012). The antecedents and
    consequences of interpersonal forgiveness: A meta-
    analytic review. *Personal Relationships*, 19(2), 304-325. doi:
    10.1111/j.1475-6811.2011.01363.x

25 Toussaint, L.L., Williams, D.R., Musick, M.A., & Everson,
    S.A. (2001). Forgiveness and health: Age differences in a
    U.S. probability sample. *Journal of Adult Development*, 8(4),
    249. doi: 10.1023/A:1011394629736

26 Pearce, M., Haynes, K. Rivera, N.R. (2018). Spiritually
    integrated cognitive processing therapy: A new treatment
    for post-traumatic stress disorder that targets moral
    injury. *Global Advances in Health and Medicine*, (7), doi.
    org/10.1177/2164956118759939

27 Legaree, T., Turner, J., & Lollis, S. (2007). Forgiveness and
    therapy: a critical review of conceptualizations, practices,
    and values found in the literature. *Journal of Marital
    and Family Therapy*, 33(2), 192-213. doi:10.1111/j.1752-
    0606.2007.00016.x

28 Nuwer.R. (2018, 16 October). Zimbabwe is pioneering a groundbreaking mental health program – with stunning results – and the rest of the world is taking note. *BBC.com.* Retrieved from https://www.bbc.com/future/article/20181015-how-one-bench-and-a-team-of-grandmothers-can-beat-depression

29 Jones, Rachel A. (2007). *You eat beans!: Kin-based joking relationships, obligations, and identity in urban Mali.* Retrieved from https://digitalcommons.macalester.edu/anth_honors/2

जी 9-18-21

Made in the USA
San Bernardino, CA
16 July 2020